Book Of Mulligan

Book Of Mulligan
18 Guaranteed Ways To Lower Your Golf Score Today

Michael Neal and Louis Faust III

iUniverse, Inc.
New York Lincoln Shanghai

Book Of Mulligan
18 Guaranteed Ways To Lower Your Golf Score Today

Copyright © 2007 by Michael Neal and Louis Faust III

All rights reserved. No part of this book may be used or reproduced by any means, graphic, electronic, or mechanical, including photocopying, recording, taping or by any information storage retrieval system without the written permission of the publisher except in the case of brief quotations embodied in critical articles and reviews.

iUniverse books may be ordered through booksellers or by contacting:

iUniverse
2021 Pine Lake Road, Suite 100
Lincoln, NE 68512
www.iuniverse.com
1-800-Authors (1-800-288-4677)

This is a work of fiction. All of the characters and events portrayed in this book are fictional. Any resemblance to real people, incidents, or especially animals is purely coincidental.

The views expressed in this work are solely those of the author and do not necessarily reflect the views of the publisher, and the publisher hereby disclaims any responsibility for them.

Illustrations by Plinio Marcos Pinto.

Visit www.bookofmulligan.com

ISBN: 978-0-595-44427-4 (pbk)
ISBN: 978-0-595-88755-2 (ebk)

Printed in the United States of America

Contents

Foreword ix
Introduction xi

Chapter 1 Get Off to a Good Start 1
    The First Tee Mulligan 2

Chapter 2 Golf Balls Don't Float 5
    The Water Mulligan 6

Chapter 3 Balance Is Key to Your Swing 9
    The Wallet Mulligan 10

Chapter 4 Ill-placed Course Obstructions 13
    The Sprinkler Head Mulligan 14

Chapter 5 Shaking on the Green 17
    The Earthquake Mulligan 18

Chapter 6 Not Measuring Up 21
    The Equipment Mulligan 22

Chapter 7 Is Your Golf Shirt Too Tight? 27
    The Clothing Mulligan 28

Chapter 8 Sand in Your Eye 31
    The Sand Mulligan 33

Chapter 9 Fuel for the Body 35
    The Blood Sugar (BS) Mulligan 36

Chapter 10 Memories	39
The At-the-Turn Mulligan	41
Chapter 11 Killer Bees	43
The Insect Mulligan	44
Chapter 12 Uncontrollable Emotions	47
The Teary-Eyed Mulligan	48
Chapter 13 When Playing Partners Distract You	51
The Etiquette Mulligan	52
Chapter 14 Physics of the Golf Ball	55
The Dimple Mulligan	56
Chapter 15 Animal Kingdom	59
The Gopher Mulligan	60
Chapter 16 Mother Nature	63
The Weather Mulligan	64
Chapter 17 Those Who Master Words	67
The Political Mulligan	68
Chapter 18 Last Resort	71
The Desperation Mulligan	72
Chapter 19 All Good Things	75
Know Your Priorities	76
Emergency Mulligan List	78
Weather Mulligans	78
Personality Mulligans	79
Seasonal Mulligans	80
Celebrity Mulligans	80
Geography Mulligans	81
Musical Mulligans	82
More Political Mulligans	83
Corporate Mulligans	84

The Final Word 86
The Lost Rule 13b 87

Foreword

I have theories about everything in golf. Well, almost. I had no theory on the mulligan. My formative rounds were played in Scotland (the land of golf but not the land of mulligan) and the reigning joke on that blessed bit of links terra firma was this:

Q: What do you call a mulligan at St. Andrews?
A: A three.

So regrettably, I had no knowledge of the Book of Mulligan.

Imagine my shock to be playing back in the states with gentlemen I did not know, usually claiming to be an 18, when they called the mulligan into play. I must digress here and explain that one of my most basic theories about golf (kind of like the Car Talk Guys theory that every woman who drives a Trans Am is named Donna) has to do with the number 18. Whenever a man tells you he is an 18, he is lying. Something about the number, not too good or too bad, just, well, untrue. Every man I have ever played with who claims to be an 18, resorts heavily on the *Book of Mulligan* or the *Book of Enron*.

Most men, I notice, also get a bit perturbed when we women putt out. I can only attribute this infuriation to the fact that they then feel compelled to follow our lead and putt out as well, thus resulting, alas, in a REAL score. (Sorry guys.)

And speaking of real scores, sometimes it takes more than bold iron play and laser-like putting to reign triumphant. But now with this little book in my library, I have enough knowledge of the mulligan and its myriad of applications that I can mount a formative defense and hold onto my cash. Of course, I write about golf for a living, so that's not saying much.

Hats off to Mr. Faust and Mr. Neal for uncovering this rare and useful information. I find it as helpful as any book on golf instruction I've ever read. And I mean that sincerely. I do grudgingly admit that Stewie is one foxy guy who used his noggin to cash in when his skill was not up to the task. And I kind of wish he were still around so I could hook him up in a foursome with George W.

Play on.

Kate Meyers

Kate Meyers is a freelance golf writer who lives in Colorado. Ms. Myers writes about people, places, and golf. Her work has appeared in Chicken Soup for the Golfer's Soul—The 2nd Round, *Golf, Golf Digest, Links, Golf Living, In Style, Life, Entertainment Weekly, Fortune and Sports Illustrated.*

Introduction

Stewart J. Mulligan lived a mostly uneventful life in Ireland until the early 1890s. Little is known about his time there other than he came from a small town south of Dublin called Bray. In his early twenties, he tended bar at a pub in Dublin until he decided one day, quite suddenly, to go to America.

Stewie, as his friends liked to call him, moved to Boston and wandered from job to job for several years until he ended up at the Franklin Park Golf Course in Dorchester soon after it opened in 1896. He started as a groundskeeper and managed to play golf in his spare time. For reasons unknown, he acquired enough money to quit his job as groundskeeper and become a full time member and player in 1904. There were rumors that he made considerable money from the various wagers he made with his fellow golfers. However, this was never proven. We do know that he became an accomplished golfer in his own right and placed second or third in twelve club championships.

Stewie was just under six feet tall and was a muscular man throughout his life. However, he was also a gentle and charismatic man who easily made friends. He was intelligent, especially when it came to understanding the complexities of dealing with people. This served him well through the years as you are about to learn.

Regardless of how Stewie made the transition from poor Irish immigrant to the life of leisure, it is the latter part of his life of which much is now known. In 2003, a dirty, moldy old notebook was discovered by Mulligan's great grandson Lewie J. The notebook Lewie discovered contained the secrets of his ancestor's successes in winning almost every informal, pick-up match for cash he played. This notebook has been carefully edited and synthesized to create the *Book of Mulligan*, making Stewie's secrets available to every golfer in the world.

A study of *The Book of Mulligan* is now required reading for all those who toil to find that one, two, or twenty shots they want to remove from their scorecard. On these pages you will find Mulligan's rule interpretations and his guide to start lowering your score today.

It is clear from a detailed review of Stewie's notebook that his strengths included more than a pretty good golf swing. He was blessed with an unusual ability to persuade others that he had superior knowledge in a variety of subjects including the rules of golf. He also could instantly assess the intelligence and knowledge of a potential playing opponent—usually following an assessment of the money said opponent had to lose. It was the combination of these skills which allowed Stewie to become a wealthy man later in life.

It is also the mastery of one of these skills that will provide you the key to lowering your score: the ability to convince your partners that you know the rules of golf better than they do. Don't worry if you are not blessed with this gift of gab. You don't need to travel to Ireland to kiss the Blarney Stone. It is your fortune that a bit of that blarney has been brought to you from Ireland courtesy of Stewie's notebook.

The first and most important lesson is that a well-used mulligan is your key to success. Actually, this is the only lesson you need. This book will teach you many different and sophisticated mulligans. It will provide their explanation and application so that you can quote them with a confidence sure to convince the most reluctant member of your foursome. You also will be provided with the historical roots for these rules so that you can share this information in the unlikely event that one of your playing partners dares question your newfound expertise.

The basis for all of these rules is the discovery in Stewie's notebook of the Lost Rule13b from the original rules of golf. Since you undoubtedly already know every rule by heart, you know that Rule 13 from the United States Golf Association is "Ball Played as it Lies." Fortunately for us, Stewie found the original Rule 13 on his travels throughout Scotland during his youth. After studying the entire text Stewie had diligently reproduced in his notebook, we realized a great injustice has been done to all golfers who do not possess the skills necessary to hit great shots every time. Yes, that is you.

It is now clear that the current Rule 13 is only half of the story. It seems that the play-the-ball-as-it-lies nonsense was actually Rule 13a. And, of course, we have Rule 13b for you here:

> Rule 13b *If after due consideration of playing the ball as it lies, and the player determines the lie of the ball is not optimum, or would not be if the ball were found, the player may consider several factors leading to the lie as shown in Rule 13b subsections, thus allowing the player to drop another ball and play without penalty.*

Stewie managed to scribe all the specifics of Rule 13b with their explanations and usage histories in his notebook. It is that knowledge which is provided to you in the following pages. Each chapter will display one of these lost subsections, the history of Stewie's use of it from his notebook, and tips on how to "apply" the rule to your game.

Once you master Mulligan's rules and interpretations, your score will drop dramatically. You will not have to spend hours on the range, pay exorbitant rates for lessons, watch any more instructional videos, or buy any more rescue clubs. All you have to do is read, study, and faithfully use the *Book of Mulligan*.

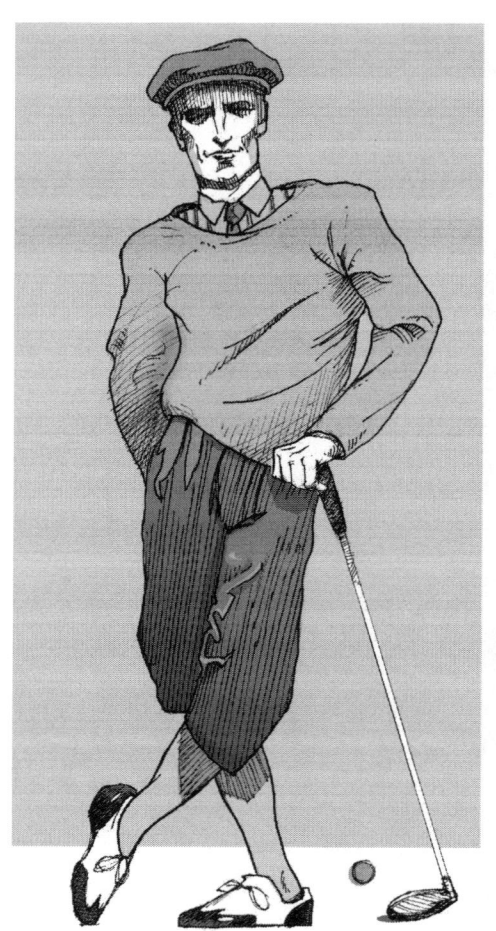

1
Get Off to a Good Start

Rule 13b.1 *Upon striking the ball on the 1st tee and determining that the ball has not come to rest in a desirable location, the player may tee up and hit another ball without penalty.*

Stewie, like all of us, had a regular group of friends he played with. It is not known how much he used his rules when he played with this group, but we do know that he would quickly excuse himself from their regular game if he could play visitors to the club for cash or refreshments.

We know from numerous notations in Stewie's notebook that the first few holes of the round were critical in determining the outcome. The process of assessing your new opponents' skills, determining their knowledge of the rules, and even observing their actual golf skills needs to be done quickly for you to develop your, um, strategy for the round.

The first objective in trying to appear both sincere and knowledgeable in any endeavor is to correctly assess the intelligence of your competitors. While there are no absolute rules used to determine your playing opponents' susceptibility to your rules interpretations, Stewie seemed to have this skill mastered. Stewie's notebook called this rating the opponents' "GA" for gullibility assessment.

Stewie divided professions into categories for his GA assessment. It is unclear how he derived these categories other than from experience with these professionals both on and off the golf course.

Stewie appears to have enjoyed playing most with doctors and lawyers. One obvious reason is that these professionals usually had money. Another belief is that he used his humble and simple speech to appear sincere and honest, while deftly applying the rules from his notebook.

It appears that doctors were the easiest to beat as they almost always seemed distracted by someone complaining about a pain here or a pain there. Lawyers might not have a high GA, but they certainly understood the concept and tried to one up Stewie after they determined his scoring "style." Unfortunately for them, Stewie was clearly the master, even on that fateful day of his first contest.

Stewie's success on the golf course can be traced back to a round played one cool September afternoon in 1904. Stewie was still a groundskeeper when three lawyers arrived at the course to play. It was a little cooler than normal and their fourth was a no show. Since club rules required a foursome, Stewie was drafted to play with this trio.

The actual events of that round are not known to this day, but Stewie was seen drinking with the three lawyers at the clubhouse and later that night at the old pub in the city where he used to work. It was a few short weeks after this episode that Stewie quit as groundskeeper and became a member at the Franklin Park Golf Course.

The First Tee Mulligan

The easiest mulligan to take is the First Tee Mulligan. Many players already know and use this mulligan, and you will likely be allowed to take it without question. However, if there is any way you can manage to hit a usable shot on the 1st tee, it is always best to let your playing partners use their mulligans. This approach will make it more difficult for them to later tell you that you cannot use one of Stewie's more creative mulligans.

The 1st tee is the place to begin working on lowering your score for the day. As we said before, your best bet to achieve success is simply by becoming the master of sincerity. Unfortunately, golfers are often compared to fisherman and politicians when trying to appear sincere.

How do you overcome this unfair bias? Let's face it; rules are made to be interpreted. Why else do we have a Supreme Court in the United States? You simply need to convince your playing partners that you are the Supreme Court of golf rules. Master sincerity, commit Stewie's notebook to memory, and your score will drop.

One particularly effective method is to practice sincerity while shaving or doing any other activity in front of a mirror. For example, you might try to say with a straight face "I did not have golf relations with that ball" or "Even though we never found any golf balls, we know that they are there." Remember, you have to convince yourself before you can convince others.

2

Golf Balls Don't Float

Rule 13b.2 Upon arriving at a water hazard and discovering the ball has entered the hazard, and, after declaring to your playing partners a sincere belief that the ball had not entered the hazard, the player may drop another ball and hit again without penalty.

Stewie did well enough for himself in his new "profession" that he made a return trip to Ireland in 1912. It is believed that he went to the south of Dublin to find his old school flame and bring her back to Boston. He had evidently booked passage to New York on a new luxury liner to impress her.

It is not known, however, what happened when Stewie arrived. The only accounts of that trip come from a few scribbled notations in a letter he sent to a Boston friend. He said it took him five days to find her and that she had just become engaged to his old best friend. Stewie seemed to take the news well but proceeded to travel from pub to pub for two weeks. He missed the departure of the new liner by a mere thirty minutes.

Since Stewie missed the boat, he decided to roam around Ireland for two weeks playing golf and visiting pubs. He found his newly acquired golfing skills did quite well. In another letter sent to a friend at Franklin Park, he discussed how easy it was to use his rules in his native land. He evidently managed to convince many players of the "American Option" for scoring. Since he also had a fair amount of wealth by now, he told them he was the inventor of the Stewie Modified Scoring System. This is how he made his money in the United States. And, you know, he was right!

After two weeks, Stewie returned to Dublin and attended the wedding of his old girlfriend and newly reinstated best friend. How could Stewie hold a grudge when he had just made so much money? It was at this wedding that Stewie met his future wife, Mary, whom he married the next day!

Once Stewie and Mary returned to Boston, he heard the news of the fate of that new ship, the Titanic. He was obviously shaken, but he did not waste time in determining how to make a near miss at death into something that could benefit him on the golf course.

It seems that whenever Stewie approached a water hazard and could not find his ball, he began to cry. It was not so much that he was sad his ball had landed in the water as much as that sad, sad, story of his lost love on the Titanic. Okay, so Stewie took liberties with the basic facts, but the story always won him sympathy and allowed him to take another shot, free of penalty!

The Water Mulligan

It is odd that golf balls don't float when virtually every other kind of ball does. The game would be much different if you could use your great shot making skills to bounce your ball off the water to a choice location on the fairway or green. You might even try this one on your playing partners if your ball manages to find water, but we doubt you will have success with this explanation—at least we have not!

We recommend you miss the water when possible, but if you happen to just barely roll from the middle of the fairway into a water hazard, have no fear. Stewie's notebook is here. While it is not likely that you can use the story that you lost your love on the Titanic, here is an opportunity to explore your inner creative self.

One tip that may work is to claim you are about to become a world-renowned golf course designer. After all, look at all the great golfers who have become designers: Nicklaus, Trevino, Norman, etc. Since you are also a great golfer (stay with us), you too can become a great designer.

Now that you have established yourself as a great course architect, start to pick apart the poor design of the course you are playing—unless it was done by one of the aforementioned greats. In that case, you need to just play better.

One method is to stop and look, more like ponder, the layout of the hole after you realize your ball has found water. Just what was that course designer thinking when he put a lake where your ball would land? Isn't it hard enough to hit a great golf shot without all those water hazards around? It is time to take back golf sanity from those evil course designers. This logic will work well if your partners have also landed in the water, perhaps not so well if their balls are sitting up on the green.

3

Balance Is Key to Your Swing

Rule 13b.3 *Upon observing the flight of the struck ball where it is determined that a player's wallet has affected the player's finely tuned balance, the player may remove the wallet, drop another ball, and hit again without penalty.*

This rule is particularly interesting given Stewie probably did not have much money in his wallet for most of his life. It is likely, however, that his wallet was heavier after a round in which his playing partners let him use this rule!

It appears Stewie first used this rule in desperation one afternoon when he was playing particularly poorly. He was playing with two appliance salesmen and was having a difficult time using any of his rule interpretations. Still, he was one shot ahead of the better player when they approached the final hole. The opponent hit a great approach and looked sure to get a birdie. Stewie had to match him, but he hit a poor approach that landed behind a tree.

Ever mindful, Stewie immediately screamed in pain and grabbed his side. The two salesmen gathered around and asked Stewie what had happened. He pulled his wallet out—which he had previously stuffed with papers surrounded by money to make it appear very fat. Stewie said the wallet had thrown his balance off and made him miss the shot and pull a muscle in his back.

The salesmen looked skeptical but, like Stewie, they were in the business of making people part with their money. They also could not help but noticing the thick wallet Stewie was brandishing.

Stewie sensed this and began to stretch out his "pulled" muscle. He asked the salesmen about their appliances and more than implied he was interested in something for his new house. This story is odd in that there is no evidence Stewie owned a house but that was not important at that moment.

After some discussion about the variety of appliances available, including a new thing called a freon-powered refrigerator, the salesmen decided to allow Stewie to hit again without a penalty. After all, they were only paying for a few beers at the clubhouse. Stewie then hit it stiff and matched the leading salesman's birdie to secure the win.

Stewie had to endure two hours of listening to the virtues of the latest appliances that 1933 had to offer, but it was made less painful given the amount of free alcohol he consumed. It is not known what became of the salesmen or how they reacted when, if ever, they discovered Stewie had never intended to buy their wares.

The Wallet Mulligan

We know from watching hours and hours of infomercials on the Golf Channel that you must have perfect balance with your swing to have the slightest hope of hitting a golf ball straight. From this indisputable fact, we then know that anything that impacts that perfect balance must, undoubtedly, cause an error in our swing. Isn't it good when science validates a mulligan?

The first tip here is to take a page from Stewie's notebook and stuff your wallet. Depending on your playing partner's financial situation, you either need to appear like you have a lot of money (stuff two twenties around twenty singles), or you will need to look like you have no money (stuff your wallet full of receipts from the pro shop). You can usually tell which scenario to play from the type of automobile the person drove up in. For players who arrive in a Mercedes, BMW, or sports cars, look like you have money. For a player dropped off by the local half-way house shuttle bus, look poor.

You may need to prepare in order to convince your partners of this rule. Once you determine that you are not playing your usual stellar game, start walking a little crooked and hunch your back. Try stretching side to side on the tee box to indicate that your back is out of whack. Ensure none of your playing partners are chiropractors before you try this one or you might get more than you bargained for.

After preparations are complete, you must decide which shot is the worst in this stretch. Perhaps you had a vision on the last green and saw that you are about to finally hit a good one. If so, wait until your next bad shot—often just your next shot—and claim the Wallet Mulligan.

Do not wait for anyone to acknowledge you, but quickly pull the wallet out of your pocket, hold it in the air for everyone to see how thick it is, and then drop it into your bag with one hand. With the other hand quickly drop another ball and hit it. You will have successfully completed a Wallet Mulligan.

4

Ill-placed Course Obstructions

Rule 13b.4 *Upon arriving to find the ball is not located in the center of the fairway, and determining that there is a sprinkler head within fifty yards of the ball, the player may assert that the ball hit the sprinkler head and move the ball into the center of the fairway and hit again without penalty.*

Since Stewie spent years as a groundskeeper at Franklin Park Golf Course, it made sense that he knew every obstruction and obstacle on the course. This inside knowledge proved to be of great benefit when he played visitors. He could state with authority the local rules.

Fortunately for us, Stewie's notebook has more references to course obstructions than anything else. Granted, Stewie considered trees, even if they were out of bounds, to be course obstructions. Stewie states in several passages that golf is a game meant to test one's ability to hit a ball straight. If, in the process of hitting a ball where you mean to, it hits something or lands behind something, then it is "obstructed" and the golfer has the right to place the ball for this unfortunate occurrence.

Stewie, always one to press an advantage, once claimed that a person was a course obstruction when he hit into a group of slow players one day. He tried to claim they purposely threw his ball into a sand trap, but his playing partners all claimed they did not see it. Stewie feigned anger and outrage and then stated that if his ball hit them and "bounced awkwardly" into the trap, then he could place his ball in the fairway where it would have naturally landed.

The partners were skeptical, but Stewie was insistent and continued to loudly contest the point. The partners finally acquiesced and Stewie placed his ball in the fairway and went on to win the hole. The partners complained all the way to the clubhouse where, as usual with Stewie, they had to buy the drinks.

The Sprinkler Head Mulligan

Stewie might not have hit many sprinkler heads in the early part of the twentieth century, but you have an opportunity to hit them all. Don't let it be lost on your playing partners the great skill this takes—hitting a small round, plastic obstacle from over 200 yards. You may even push your luck and tell them you get a bonus mulligan for hitting the sprinkler head even if your ball is theoretically "lost."

This is another of those rules you should prepare your playing partners for early in the round. Some tips include pointing out your deep understanding of how sprinkler heads are arranged on the course, how newer technology sprinkler heads do not require that huge plastic, obstructing cover, and how useless it is to put yardage on sprinkler heads now that you have your GPS-enabled, laser range finder in your air-conditioned golf cart. The point here is to create ill will towards the sprinkler head. Give it a negative persona.

A good time to use the Sprinkler Head Mulligan is when your competitors cannot see the ball landing area or they see your ball jump high in the air after it lands. Now fight the temptation to allow them to tell you that the ball hit the cart path and bounced that high. After all, have you ever seen a paved cart path in the middle of the fairway where your ball always lands?

As always, be vigilant and ready. If you can detect immediately after your shot that it might not have been your best effort, exclaim "Wow, that felt good to absolutely hammer the ball down the middle like that!" Try not to make eye contact even if you sense disbelief from anyone in your foursome.

Now that you have properly set expectations about where your ball will be found, concentrate on locating the sprinkler head in the fairway as you finish walking 300 yards from the tee. By now, all of your weaker hitting competitors have hit their second shots and you will know how much you need to press this rule. If they are in trouble, you can find the closest hazard still nearer the green and take a drop from it since your ball obviously skipped off the sprinkler head an additional fifty yards.

If someone is close and you are in danger of losing the hole, press hard that the local course rules do not penalize you for your massive, straight drive that hit the oversized and obstructive sprinkler head. Even if you lose this point, make sure you wear down the fighting will of these insensitive golfers as that, at least, may come in handy later (see Chapter 18—Last Resort).

5

Shaking on the Green

Rule 13b.5 Upon observing a putted ball that takes an unexplained break, and the player determines that a mild earthquake just occurred, even if not all playing partners felt the earth shaking, or you are within 1000 miles of California, the player may putt again without penalty.

Stewie grew up in Ireland and lived all of his life on the United States East Coast, so it was interesting that his notebook contained references to earthquakes. After additional research deep into the yellowing pages of the notebook, it was discovered that Stewie took a trip to San Francisco in April of 1906.

Stewie had played two rounds that day and evidently done well. He and his playing partners were out late visiting nightclubs when Stewie ran out of money around 5:00 a.m. He was able to convince someone to bet him he could make a putt across the tavern floor. Just as he putted, the big one hit. The putt missed and Stewie was of sufficient mind to loudly call Earthquake Mulligan. The tavern had cleared by then and Stewie simply took his drink from behind the counter as a debt unpaid.

Stewie had a round set up for 11:00 the next morning with the reining San Francisco Bay area club champion. The champ made the tee time but was obviously frazzled by the earthquake and aftershocks. Stewie played him even until the 18th hole by evoking many of his East Coast rules.

The champ missed his long birdie putt and Stewie had a 20 foot bender to win the match outright. Just as his putt slid to the right of the hole, Stewie fell down and exclaimed that the shaking earth had knocked him over and made his ball miss. He explained that he was entitled to a re-putt based on the earthquake. Before anyone could object, Stewie dropped his ball and sent the next putt dead center into the hole, winning the match.

The Earthquake Mulligan

If you live in California, this mulligan is almost too easy to claim. If not, we have tips for you to employ in that rare case where your playing partners have an IQ. Speaking of intelligence, which is directly related to a player's GA, make sure there are no geologists in the foursome before pressing this point.

In fact, especially if you are a terrible putter or you choke a lot, you might want to establish yourself as a world famous geologist so you can use several of these rules to your advantage. You should say that you are completing your second Ph.D in Geology. Your dissertation topic is *The Effect of Abnormally High Grass Watering on Plate Tectonics*. Hopefully your playing partners ask what plate tectonics are and you can explain they are the moving of the earth's surface. Explain to them, that while they may know about California they might not be aware that earthquakes occur throughout the world on a daily basis, including, oddly enough, under golf courses.

If you feel adventurous or think your competitors might be a little smarter than you would like, we recommend you carry a small compass in your bag. After talking about earthquakes for a few holes, you can take advantage of your next missed putt to claim the Earthquake Mulligan. Quickly pull the compass from your bag and show how the magnetic poles have become disorientated, which indicate that an earthquake has just occurred. If your opponents appear skeptical, take out a pad of paper or a napkin and begin to make notes on the date, time, sun angle, and compass readings on the notepad. Note: it will be more convincing if you already had similar notations on the paper.

If you don't have a compass, try using almost anything with the explanation above. After all, it makes as much sense to show this with a pencil as a compass.

6

Not Measuring Up

Rule 13b.6 *Upon observing the flight of a well struck ball which goes astray, resembling a hook or a slice, when it is determined that the player rarely, if ever, hits a hook or a slice, the player may inspect his club to determine if it has a defect, and, finding a defect, may drop a ball, choose another club, and hit again without penalty.*

You might think from watching politicians and corporate executives these days that we live in a time of excuses. You can rest assured that these guys have nothing over Stewie. When all else fails, Stewie had one no-fail rule in his bag—so to speak.

Interestingly, the first discussions about rules interpretations in Stewie's notebook are about equipment malfunctions (see Chapter 7 for wardrobe malfunctions). The use of this rule appears to have one peculiar aspect that makes it stand out from the others. It appears that this mulligan was not originally Stewie's invention—we mean from the Lost Rule 13b. This rule came from a playing partner in 1919. The young man was a pitcher for the local sports team. He had become a hero when they won their title in 1918, but he was despondent when they lost the next year.

One late afternoon in 1919, the young man came out to Franklin Park. He was very upset and wanted to play a quick round of golf. It seems he had become agitated because he had been traded to the dreaded rival. There were not many people around, so Stewie agreed to go with him as a twosome for a quick round. They were able to get the foursome rule waived since the starter was a big baseball fan.

The poor baseball player was tied with Stewie as they stood over their second shot on the 18th hole. He hit a terrible shot and immediately claimed he had a broken club and was due another shot. Stewie later recalled that he did not challenge the despondent man because he was having such a good round, a tie was the worst he could do. He also liked the young baby-faced baseball player.

It is not clear from the notebook who bought the drinks in the clubhouse later, but the pair ended up at the local baseball park late that evening. Since Stewie knew the groundskeeper, an old Franklin Park groundskeeper from Stewie's earlier days, they managed to talk their way inside and sat down near home plate.

Fortunately, there was a full moon to light the night sky, and Stewie began hitting golf balls into the stands. The pitcher wandered over and picked up a bat and started belting balls into the stands as well. Stewie's notes say he told the young man he should consider giving up pitching and concentrate on hitting. The young man paused and thanked Stewie for the tip.

As the night grew late, the young man suddenly jumped up and drilled one last ball deep into the stands. He yelled, "Curse you, Red Sox. You won't win another World Series until the next century!"

Stewie looked up at the bright moon and said quietly, "Good one, Bambino."

The Equipment Mulligan

The Equipment Mulligan was much easier for Stewie to claim in the days of woodies and imperfect balls. Admittedly, it will be difficult to claim poor equipment when you have six months of your salary sitting in your bag: graphite shafts, oversized heads, special weighting, adjustable weighting, specially designed two ball putters, and no spin, no slice, soft feel, long distance balls. Still, you may be able to claim this rule with a little ingenuity. You will just have to be more creative.

Since golf ball technology has reached the point that it seems the balls can almost drive themselves down the fairway, it will be difficult for you to claim a problem with your ball. That leaves your clubs, glove, and bag. Hey, don't rule out the impact your bag has on your swing!

Your glove could have an impact, but your competitors can always tell you to take it off. They can't tell you, however, not to use your clubs. Since there is one club you can surely blame for many, many shots, let's start there. The putter, of course, is the best choice for poor equipment issues. You only have one in your bag, it is used on every hole, and it can have a wide variety of problems—many of them unseen until they cause you to miss that key putt.

One issue in using this rule is that you must be able to convince your worthy competitors that the club defect is real. There are several ways to do this, but we have found (we mean heard) that the most successful way is to carry small tools with you to mark the club to simulate, actually highlight, the club's defect. Another advantage of having tools is that you can claim you fixed the malfunction if by some miracle you make a putt on the next hole.

If you are tool-challenged like you are golf-challenged, then you have to take another approach. Hopefully, by now, you have mastered the art of appearing sincere and credible even if you are not a particular expert on a topic. For an Equipment Mulligan, you should immediately call the mulligan after you notice the shot has unexpectedly gone astray. Take off your glove and hat, raise the club high in the air, and slowly rotate the club as you peer down the shaft.

Your playing partners will likely become suspicious at this point. You must ignore them and remain focused on examining the club in question. Once enough time has passed that you feel comfortable, let out a slow and deliberate "Ummmmmm" sound. Then say something to the effect that you suspected this hairline fracture, soft mold, manufacturing problem. You might tell a story about the time you visited the actual plant where your clubs were made and toured the assembly line with the CEO. You were impressed with the technology, but you were concerned about that one stage of the manufacturing process.

As you near the end of the story, peek out the corner of your eye to see if your playing partners are buying this. If not, we recommend you pass on this mulligan.

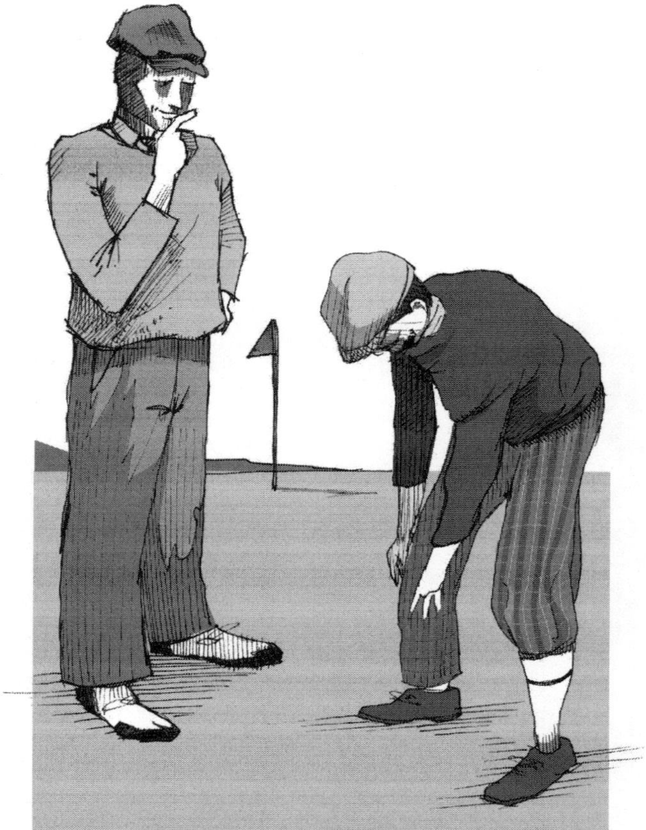

7

Is Your Golf Shirt Too Tight?

> Rule 13b.7 *Upon striking a shot that does not travel in the intended direction and upon a determination by the player that an article of clothing interfered with the player's natural swing motion, the player may drop a ball and hit again without penalty.*

Ireland, Stewie's home, is known for its rugged weather. When Stewie came to America and settled in the Boston area he had no idea what the weather would bring. He was quickly and rudely introduced to the bitter cold New England winters (See Chapter 16—Mother Nature). The Boston winter soon made Stewie long for the winters of his homeland.

To play in such conditions required thought in terms of what golfers should wear. In the fall and winter, golfers would be bundled up to such a degree to protect themselves from the rain and wind and snow that it was often hard to even grip the golf club.

Summer provided a respite. One of those fine summer days, Stewie was playing with three other members of the club, all of whom were nattily attired in their Sunday best and fit for the fashion papers of their day. In fact, this particular group of three, who always played together, was known amongst the club members as The Three Fashioneers since fashion was their true calling. Stewie was always amused by their outfits.

This particular day, one of the Three Fashioneers, Mikie Tartan, was deeply troubled by the winds, which kept whipping his pants legs around. To eliminate this constant distraction, Mikie bent down and tucked his pant legs into his socks. What no one knew at the time was that by doing this, Mikie Tartan later became known as the inventor of the Plus Fours made popular decades later by such golfing stars as Payne Stewart, the 1999 U.S. Open champion.

Stewie, upon witnessing this, created what has now become known as the "Clothing Mulligan." When Stewie first invoked this mulligan, his playing partners protested, as they inevitably did whenever Stewie announced a new rule. However, as with all of Stewie's rules, he was able to persuade his fellow competitors of the logic of his view and, thus, the protests were ultimately to no avail.

The Clothing Mulligan

Planning for that timely wardrobe malfunction may be difficult in a sport whose uniform is traditionally just pants, shoes, and a loose fitting golf shirt. However, you may, like many players these days, also include an expensive hat proclaiming your latest course conquest or tournament attended. With so few choices for blaming (we mean explaining) a poor shot, you may have trouble using this gem. However, as always, we have some ideas.

First, you should not try to invent an obvious or silly mulligan. This approach would break your streak of using the highly sophisticated, classic mulligans described thus far in this book. Let's start by eliminating the following no-chance mulligans:

- My hat was crooked
- My belt was too tight
- My socks have slipped down

Simply said, these mulligans lack imagination.

We are assuming, in general, that you are a little older than the average golfer. We think younger people still live under the illusion that they can actually learn this confounding game and don't think they need Stewie's rules.

You, however, obviously understand the game and, as with all such astute players, are searching for anything to give you an edge. Why else would you have read this far? So, we have a strategy that might be a little risky for you, might subject you to some ridicule from your competitors, but ultimately might prove successful.

We would like you to dress like a Hip Hop Artist. If you don't know what that means, don't worry. We are here to help. After all, what better source of hip hop expertise could there be than from two middle-aged-white guys?

First, look in the mirror at how you dress: Think about how the oversized clothing and large jewelry (a.k.a. "Bling") could interfere with your finely honed swing. If you do not have any bling to wear, try using an old putter head on a chain. It is best to glue a little gold dust on it for the right effect.

Second, you need a good stage name. Even though it seems all of the good names are taken, you might try to use a variation like Raspberry T, Notoriously Small, or Snoopy Cat.

Finally, work on your lingo. You don't need to be an expert, but you don't want to embarrass yourself in case your playing partners either know Hip Hop or have kids who do. For example, Eminem is not a candy—he is a Rap Artist.

Note: if you still don't have a clue about Hip Hop or Rap, maybe you should pass on this one. You have too far to go. If you are otherwise musically inclined, though, you can still find help in the Emergency Mulligan List under Musical Mulligans.

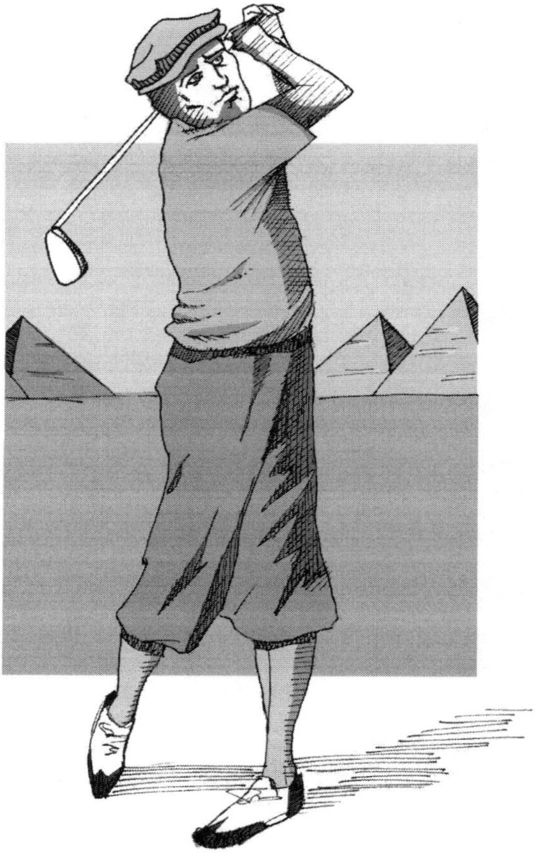

8

Sand in Your Eye

> Rule 13b.8 *Upon striking a ball in a sand trap and the ball lands either in the same sand trap, a different sand trap, or in any location other than on the intended green, the player may elect to drop a ball no closer to the hole and hit again without penalty.*

The Sand Mulligan was perhaps Stewie's ultimate challenge. Most players know the rules for playing out of a sand trap: you cannot ground your club, you cannot move the ball out of a footprint, you cannot use your foot wedge to move the ball to the grass, etc. However, anyone who knew Stewie accepted it was only a matter of time before he would come up with something to help his merely average sand skills.

As we said earlier, little was known of Stewie's life in Ireland. However, in researching this book, more came to be known about his time before he came to America. Stewie's sense of adventure that led him to pack up and leave for America turned out not to be his first foreign adventure.

Stewie, it seems, went to Africa in his late teenage years. While in Africa, Stewie became enamored with local customs and practices. As you might imagine, an Irishman in Africa in the 1890's was quite a rare sight.

One night while drinking with several friends, Stewie got himself into a bit of trouble with the local officials. He was able to get out of the situation that night, but several of his friends warned him that the officials would likely come after him in the next few days and he may have more trouble.

Rather than face an uncertain fate at their hands, Stewie decided to head into the desert. He quickly packed his meager possessions and left town. In doing so, he met and then joined a group of men who it turns out were mostly from France. Stewie thought they often looked like they were running from something.

Stewie ended up becoming part of this ragtag group of foreigners. They found themselves in many delicate situations where they had no choice but to fight their way out. Over time, the group became quite proficient at the ways of fighting in the desert and their reputation spread far and wide. More men from more countries heard of their exploits and joined them. The more the group grew in numbers, the more so to did their conquests and their reputations.

They may have formed quite a ragged group in the beginning. However, by the time Stewie left, this group had become known far and wide as the French Foreign Legion.

Over time, Stewie became skilled with a rifle and was known for his uncanny ability to hit a target with his shot straight down the middle. One day when he hit yet another target this way, one of his fellow marksmen dubbed him the "Straight Shooter." While we are not sure if the French really understood this idea, today, as every other golfer knows, when someone is called a "Straight Shooter" it immediately lets everyone know that this golfer is one you can trust since he calls them as he sees them.

To pass the time in the desert, Stewie began to tell the men stories. One night he introduced his fellow travelers to the game of golf as he had come to know it from the stories he had heard in the pub back home. Of course, they had no clubs with them in the African desert. So Stewie had to improvise. One thing he had an abundance of was sand. Never having played the game before and knowing only what he knew from the pub stories, Stewie never knew what he had right and what he didn't. His only saving grace was he was talking to a bunch of Frenchmen who knew even less about the game than he did. After all, name three great French golfers. Enough said.

The Sand Mulligan

Your intuition may tell you to only attempt to use this mulligan in what would commonly be called a "sand trap." What most golfers don't know, however, is that the USGA prefers the term "bunker" and not "trap." This rule was probably written by a bunch of guys who recalled their old army days where it was often good to be in a bunker when things got scary. Nowadays, it is scary to be in the bunker!

Since it is likely at some time during a round that you will end up in one of these bunkers, you need a strategy. Since most of your life spent standing in sand has been at the beach, you probably don't have the skills to actually hit a good shot here.

Let's start by stepping back and looking philosophically at the obstacle unofficially called the sand trap. Do you realize it is the only obstacle that a special club is created for? It's the original rescue club: The Sand Wedge. There is no water wedge, no out of bounds wood. Even golf club makers know the perils of this obstacle. So what are you to do?

One of your co-authors has completely given up on learning the sand game and solved this problem by using his putter to get out of traps. While that has actually worked (we think it has more to do with closing his eyes when he hits the ball), we suggest you try the traditional shot with a wedge. If by some unlucky occurrence your ball does not come to rest beside the hole, you need to resort to Rule 13b yet again.

Another consideration is the sand in general. Just what constitutes a sand trap? While the Sahara Desert may be the world's largest natural sand trap, you do not need such an expanse of sand to properly invoke the Sand Mulligan. On the surface it would appear that the interpretation of this mulligan is for the ball to be in a constructed sand trap. However, we see from Stewie's notebook it was intended for much broader use. In fact, you may properly use it as soon as you see, or even think you see, one or more grains of sand on or near your ball. This usage may require all of your oratory skills and sincerity, particularly if your competitors do not observe the same sand quotient as you. Be firm and do not hesitate. Claim your mulligan, hit again, and play on!

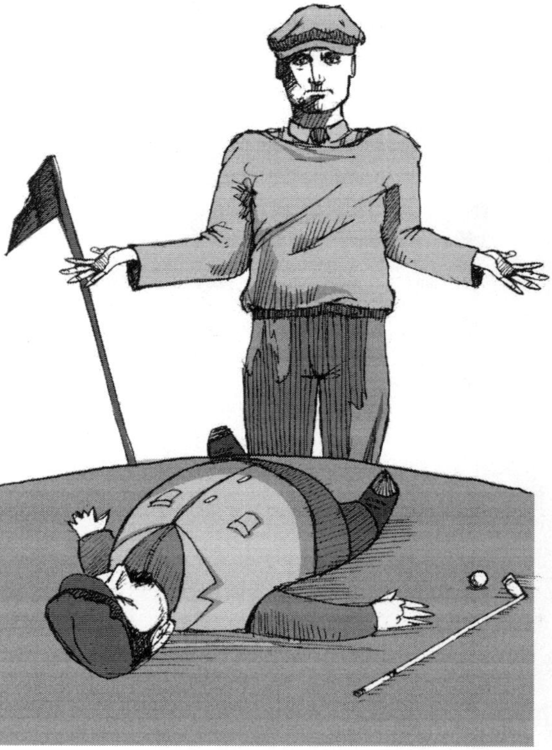

9

Fuel for the Body

> Rule 13b.9 *Upon striking a shot that does not travel the intended distance, and upon a determination by the player that said player is hungry or thirsty thus exhibiting signs of dangerously low blood sugar that clearly impairs said player's physical capability, the player may elect to drop a ball no closer to the hole, consume some combination of food and liquids, and hit again without penalty.*

Food is the fuel that powers the human engine. Stewie knew a lot about engines as one of his many odd jobs was as a mechanic before he discovered his true calling in golf. He soon became more a student of the human condition than he had been of an engine's condition. He also began to understand that a person must have the right fluids and foods in order to perform to their maximum potential. This principal was driven home to Stewie in his first club championship at Franklin Park.

In that club championship, Stewie was in the final foursome. In addition to Stewie, Mikie Tartan, Rickie Simpson, and Dickie Thompson also played. Mikie, as we know, had quite an eye for fashion. Rickie, as it happens, enjoyed his beer and had the physique to prove it. Dickie was the best pure golfer in the club and, unfortunately, he knew it and acted accordingly. He was a medical doctor. Need we say more?

During the front 9, the match was extremely close. However, beginning with the 10th hole, Rickie's play began to drop off quickly and dramatically. He fell three shots back of Dickie who had now taken a one shot lead over Stewie and two over Mikie. By the 13th hole, Rickie had to stop and rest after every shot.

Just as Stewie, Mikie and Dickie had decided to confront Rickie about his slow play, he fell to the ground, his eyes rolled back in his head, and he passed out. The three of them shook Rickie and finally were able to revive him. He woke up and said he was starving and his mouth was dry. Dickie spoke with him, asked him a number of questions, and then told Stewie and Mikie to get Rickie something to eat and drink after which he would be fine.

Stewie asked Dickie how he knew what to do. Dickie told them it was clear that Rickie was not eating or drinking enough and that his blood sugar had just dropped to a dangerous level and that what happened to him was inevitable.

Upon hearing this, Mikie was upset and accused Dickie of knowing this was happening to Rickie and then taking full advantage of it in the championship match. As Mikie fumed, Stewie put two and two together and connected what he just heard from Dickie with what he knew about engines. Fuel was required, and thus, another mulligan was born.

The Blood Sugar (BS) Mulligan

Every day in America there is a "New Life Changing Diet" that one celebrity or another seems to endorse. We have the Atkins Diet and the South Beach Diet. We have everyone from Oprah to Dr. Phil telling us what they did to lose weight and feel good. They are the perfect people to invoke what has become know as the BS Mulligan.

You may not have had the same challenges as Oprah (Oh, how we wish we had some of those challenges!), but you too can properly invoke the BS Mulligan. Again, sincerity and preparation are the keys to success.

To set up this mulligan, simply begin by discussing your weight and the latest diet you are on. Since we have observed golfers around the world, we are confident that many of you naturally qualify for this mulligan. Its beauty is that for every new diet you try, you can use this mulligan.

A recent search on Amazon.com showed there were 189,565 diet books in its system. It seems like there is a diet book for just about every way you can think of dieting. Here's just a brief sample for you to choose from (these are all REAL diets; we swear we did not make them up; we're funny but not this funny):

- The Sonoma Diet: Trimmer Waist, Better Health in Ten Days (We guess this has something to do with drinking wine since Sonoma is a wine growing region in California.)

- The Fast Track One-Day Detox Diet (When ten days are too long.)

- The 3-Hour Diet (You may be able to finish this diet before you finish your round.)

- The G.I. Diet (If you eat military rations, you are bound to lose weight.)

- The Fat Flush Plan (We don't want to think about this one.)

- The Cheater's Diet (Sounds like some golfers we have played with.)

- The Last Diet Book You'll Ever Need (Well, someone had to have the "last" word on this one.)

- The Maker's Diet (When only divine intervention will do.)

Now, since you have been physically exerting yourself walking from the golf cart to your ball, continue by telling your worthy, in-shape competitors how your diet seems to be affecting your energy level. You have now set the stage for invoking the BS Mulligan. Simply, pick the bad shot of your choice, immediately feign a collapse on the golf course after hitting it, and cry out that your blood sugar has dropped due to your diet thus causing you to mis-hit your last shot. Drop another ball and immediately hit again. It might be good to eat a banana like Tiger does when he plays. Then again, you could do just as well with a Snickers Bar.

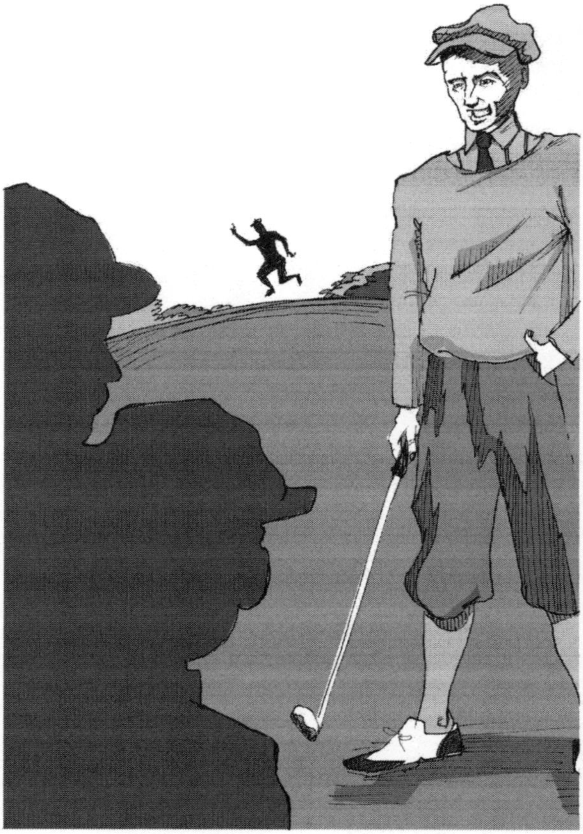

10

Memories

Rule 13b.10 *Upon completion of the first nine holes of an eighteen hole round, when the player determines that their cumulative score for said nine holes exceeds the score intended by said player, the player may, at their sole discretion, adjust said Front 9 score by one or more strokes in order to better align said player's actual score with their intended score without penalty.*

Stewie always played 18 holes of golf. He never understood people who said "Let's just play 9." To Stewie, that wasn't golf. It was some other sport. If you didn't have the time, go knit. Don't take up space from the real golfers. That was Stewie's philosophy.

Try as he would, Stewie was not always successful in ensuring that his playing partners were all planning on playing 18 holes. As word got out in the club that Stewie was only an 18 hole guy, people avoided him when they only wanted to play 9. Occasionally, others tried to trick him into playing with them even though they had no intention of playing a full 18. To some it often became as much a sport to try to trick Stewie as to play the round itself.

One day Stewie was waiting on the 1st tee with two other players waiting on a fourth when a man came up huffing and puffing and asked to join them. Stewie did not know the player but the two other members of their group said they did, so Stewie agreed to let the new player join.

It soon became clear that Stewie had been had and that the new player had no intention of playing the full 18 holes. Stewie was fuming. However, he was not about to let on to the others how he really felt. He knew instantly how he could reverse the gag on his three playing partners.

As the Front 9 progressed, Stewie was playing poorly and was losing the match. Yet he had not used any of the Mulligan Rules for which he was widely known not only within the club but throughout the greater Boston area.

His playing partners became increasingly distracted and began forgetting who had how many strokes on each hole. No one who had ever played with Stewie had gone nine holes without him invoking at least one and generally several mulligans.

The group finally teed off on the 9th hole and still no mulligans had been used by Stewie. They hit their second shots. Still no mulligan. Everyone was on the green in two and all had makeable birdie putts. Surely now was the time the three of them thought that Stewie would make his move. Nothing.

Finally, all putts were made and the Front 9 was over. None of the three players could believe what they had just seen. It was going to be the talk of the club for some time to come. Stewie had not called a single mulligan on the Front 9 that day, and there were witnesses.

As the scores were being tallied, the last minute player started to run off toward the clubhouse. Stewie became angry and shouted that the player could not leave or his score would be penalized. Then it hit him. "Actually," said Stewie with a wry Irish smile as he calmed down, "he can go."

Stewie then played his card. His scorecard. Since the foursome, a cornerstone of the game of golf, was destroyed by the departing player, and since the two remaining players knew him, Stewie reasoned he was entitled to three strokes of score "adjustment" for pain and suffering. (We see a lawyer influence creeping in here.) With that adjustment, Stewie took the lead and eventually won the round and, of course, all wagers and refreshments.

The At-the-Turn Mulligan

If you have made the turn after nine glorious holes, it can mean one of two things: either you are having the round of your life or you want another nine punishing holes to work out the minor kinks in your swing. We doubt the former, and we suspect the latter. We also doubt you only need a few slight modifications anyway. So, you will need more mulligans for the Back 9 to keep your score moving lower.

As you make the turn, it is time to take serious stock. Not of your life, but of your usage of Stewie's rules for the first half of the round. Did your worthy and honorable competitors allow you the rule interpretations you deserved? Or did they argue with you and deny you your golf-guaranteed rights?

If you have not been successful to this point, it is not going to get any easier. So why don't you actually try to play good golf instead of relying on these rules? Okay, we understand. After all, we have been trying to learn this game too.

Fortunately for you, we have another fresh set of Rule 13b subsections after the turn. First though, one key to success for winning the Back 9 is to ensure that your playing partners lose some or all of their memory of your warm up (i.e., the Front 9). We are not suggesting that you whack them on the head to induce amnesia. It does not work and just makes them mad—or so we've heard.

What we do suggest is a media campaign worthy of a U. S. President up for reelection. Start by buying alcoholic drinks, if you can. Follow up by highlighting your great shots on the Front 9. If you had no great shots, make them up. Try to have genuine excitement in your voice. Downplay, don't mention, or, better yet, forget any mulligans you may have taken. That was ancient history. Rule 13b says you can start over at the turn anyway (It really doesn't, but who cares at this point).

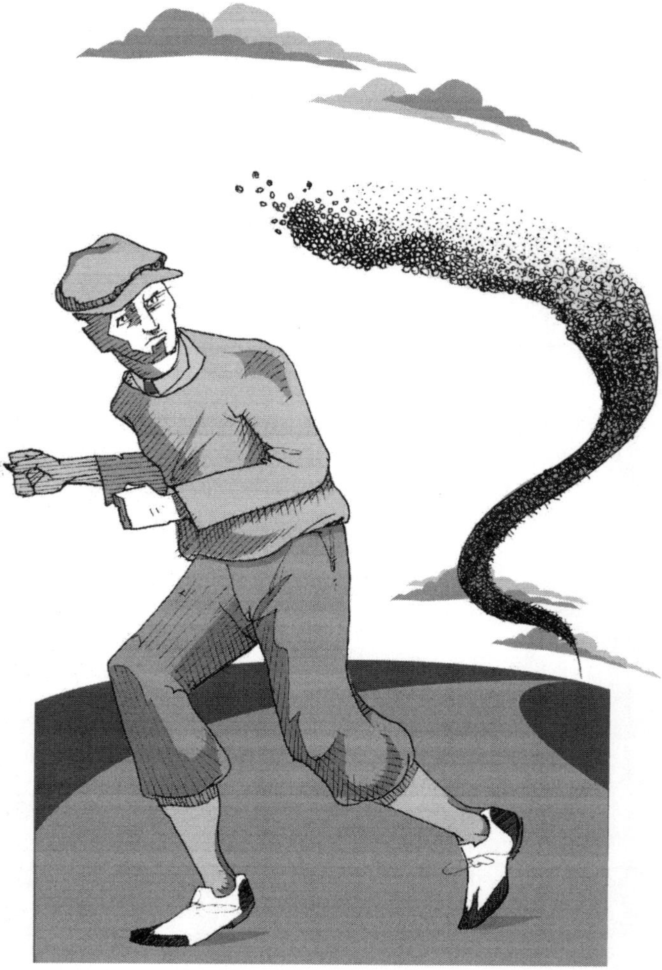

11

Killer Bees

Rule 13b.11 *Upon striking the ball in less than an optimal manner, and upon a determination by the player that such sub-optimal striking of the ball resulted from a distraction caused by an insect, such as a killer bee, the player may, at their sole discretion, drop a ball and hit again without penalty.*

Stewie traveled far and wide as we now know. He had been to Africa in his late teens and then moved to the United States in his early twenties. We also have discovered that Stewie traveled to South America soon after he came to Boston. There he was exposed to many dangerous animals and insects. As with many visitors to the rain forest, Stewie became quite paranoid about insects. He had seen people die in South America from a single bite from the wrong bug.

One day Stewie was out showing the locals how to play golf in the rain forest when they heard a loud buzzing sound. However, there was something different about it. As he listened more closely, it was unlike any sound which he had ever heard before. It increased with intensity and, when he finally realized what it was, the swarm was upon them, and it was too late to run. Suddenly, Stewie was in the middle of a cloud of bees so thick it cut off the sun's light and he was enveloped in darkness. Those around him also were surrounded and, even though they were all within a foot of each other, they could not see each other.

The swarm finally passed, and two of the people with Stewie lay on the ground—dead. At the time no one really knew why. While Stewie was covered with welts from the bites, he survived. It was only much later when Stewie was back in Boston that he would read of a new phenomenon which scientists had dubbed "Killer Bees." From that moment on, the sound of a bee caused Stewie's heart to race as it immediately brought back memories of that fateful day in the rain forest.

Over time Stewie thought less and less about the Killer Bees. However, one day when he was out on the course during the height of a hot, humid Boston summer, he heard that sound. Although he could not actually see a bee, he knew that eerie, incessant whine. That was enough. He played the rest of the round poorly and did not use his rules to lower his score. He finished the round and even skipped the clubhouse to go home.

On his next round of golf, Stewie heard the sound again and this time a real bee landed on the shaft of his putter. Stewie froze in mid-stroke and tried to break off his swing, but he touched the ball and it moved—normally a clear violation of the rules subject to a penalty. Ever quick to recover, Stewie immediately invoked the Insect Mulligan and saved himself the stroke.

The Insect Mulligan

In today's world, we face increasing threats from many sources, including insects. From the Bird Flu to the West Nile Virus, all of us need to be wary of any flying creature. The good news for golfers is that this proliferation of life threatening insects gives each of us tremendous opportunities to use this mulligan.

At any point in your round, the mere appearance of an insect provides you with an unimpeachable basis for using this mulligan. Most golf courses will be a veritable ecosystem with numerous insects and other assorted flying creatures, all of which give you many opportunities. Consequently, if you hear a bee or even just think you hear a bee without actually seeing the bee, you can still use this mulligan.

One caution, however, if any one of your playing partners is an entomologist, then be extremely careful in attempting to use this mulligan. All of the sincerity you have worked so hard to establish with your playing partners may be lost if you don't use this mulligan correctly.

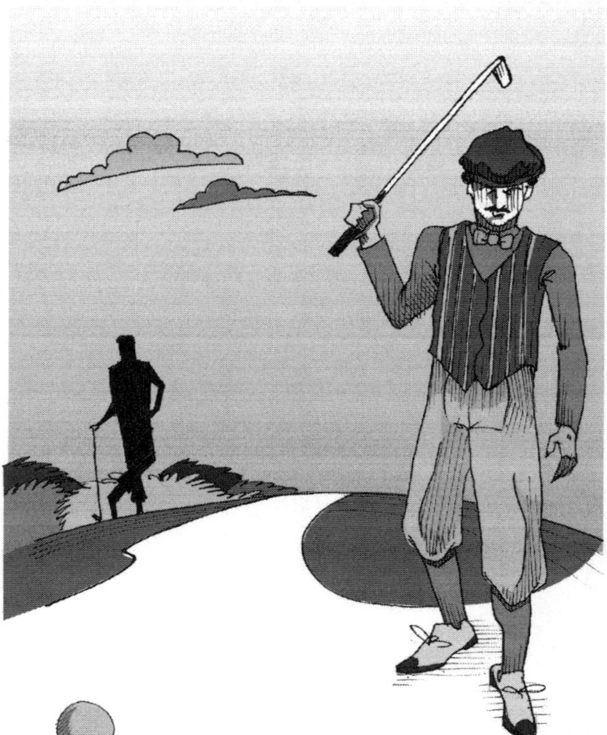

12

Uncontrollable Emotions

Rule 13b.12 Upon striking a ball and, upon a determination by the player that such shot did not travel in its intended normal, straight and long trajectory, and upon further determination that the cause of such misdirection was tears that filled the player's eyes from missing a six-inch putt on the prior green, or other equal tragedy, the player may wipe their eyes, drop another ball, and hit again without penalty.

Stewie was a stout fellow and not known for showing emotion. Many at the club thought they would not want to face him in a poker game. They could never tell what he was thinking. That suited Stewie fine. However, the club did have its share of folks who wore their emotions on their sleeves. Stewie had no patience for these people. It wasn't that he was not a sensitive man. He did have strong feelings, and, after all, he was Irish. He just thought that the golf course was not the place for such shows of emotion. But Stewie was not one to let an opportunity pass to lower his score.

One beautiful fall weekend, Stewie went to the club to play a round. He approached his buddy the starter, who placed him with a group that Stewie only knew from the bar at the club. He had never played with any of them. However, his experience with one member of this group immediately raised the hairs on the back of his neck. This person was known for indulging a bit too much in his drink and then becoming a whimpering, whining man. None of those traits were of interest to Stewie.

The group teed off and things were going well over the first several holes. Then the player Stewie dreaded began to have some problems with his game. Unfortunately, things went from bad to worse and the poor golfer was not able to do anything to stop the proverbial bleeding. Finally at the 13th hole, he missed a one foot putt that put him over the edge. He literally broke down in tears and was heard sobbing all the way to the next tee.

On the 14th hole, he finally reached the green and was about to putt when Stewie saw the tears well up in his eyes as the pressure of his last missed putt mounted. He pulled the putter back, stroked it and missed another short putt to lose the second straight hole. Feeling no sympathy for him, but not being one to look a gift horse, or putt, in the mouth, Stewie was inspired by his playing partner's misery. Later, as he enjoyed the fruits of his labor of that day, he scribbled his new creation into his notebook: a mulligan which brought years of tears of joy to his eyes.

The Teary-Eyed Mulligan

Tears can be powerful. Through the ages, tears have been shed in joy and in sorrow. Tears have been shed by children to get their way and by men and women seeking the same. In golf, it is believed, that more tears have been shed in sorrow than in joy. If you are reading this book, chances are you are one of those people who have shed such tears of sorrow.

To use the Teary-Eyed Mulligan, it is helpful if a player can summon a tear or two upon command. Again, sincerity and timing are critical to the successful use of this mulligan. Start several holes prior to invoking this mulligan. Begin by sharing your "true feelings" with your fellow players. Men, unfortunately, seem to be at a genetic disadvantage in their ability to effectively employ this mulligan. If you are playing with only other men, however, it will be just fine because to other men, it will seem sincere. However, be very careful if you have one or more women in your foursome. Any woman will spot a man's lack of sincerity from any distance less than 500 yards rendering any golf hole, except perhaps for long Par 5's, virtually unsuitable for this mulligan.

Share personal stories of tragedy or joy. Here are some examples of things that make people sad and/or happy that can be used as a basis for this mulligan:

Sad Events

- Death of a pet

- Loss of a bet

- Damage to your favorite golf club

Happy Events

- Death of a pet (you never really liked the mutt)

- Loss of a bet (rare if you use this book)

- Damage to your favorite golf club (you couldn't hit that club anyway)

You get the idea. In assessing the GA rating of your playing partners, you will be able to determine whether stories of joy or of sorrow will be the most effective.

Once you decide which story to use, as you approach the hole, begin to mutter just loud enough to be heard by your playing partners, how you cannot believe that you missed the putt on the prior hole. Then upon stroking the next putt and missing, you immediately need to be heard sniffling. Then, after pausing for dramatic effect (trust us, okay?), cry out in anguish saying something like "I can't believe that Muffy is gone. I can't stop thinking about her!" Since you have already established how sensitive you are, this cry for help will be immediately understood by your playing partners. Or they might just want to get away from you as fast as possible. No matter. Quickly call the mulligan, drop a second ball and stroke your putt. You have now successfully used the Teary-Eyed Mulligan.

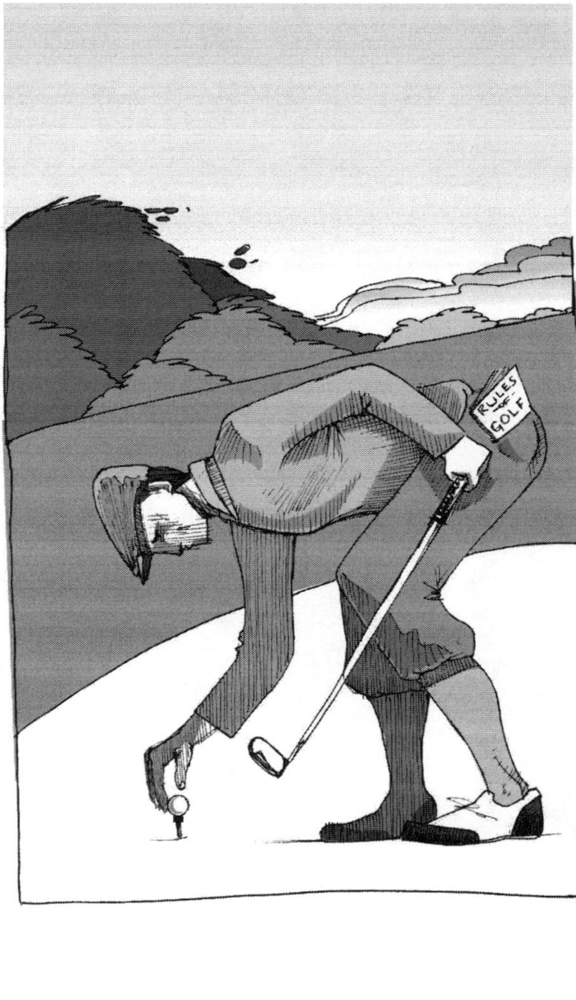
RULES
OF
GOLF

13

When Playing Partners Distract You

Rule 13b.13 *Upon striking the ball with less than the desired results, and upon determining that one of your playing partners has violated the rules of golf etiquette during your swing such as coughing, sneezing, blinking, or breathing, the player may drop another ball and hit again without penalty.*

Stewie may not have lived the refined life when he was growing up, but he managed to learn the power of embarrassment. A notation from January 1908 in Stewie's notebook describes a round he played with a portly (an early twentieth century word for "fat") gentleman who had many disgusting habits. In particular, the gentleman committed virtually every etiquette violation imaginable during the round. Stewie found this extremely irritating.

The man walked across Stewie's line on the 1st green, laughed during Stewie's swing on the 2nd tee, and was the slowest player Stewie had ever seen. Stewie was trying to maintain his Irish temper but it got the best of him at the turn when the gentleman stood only inches from the hole during a putt Stewie needed to win.

Stewie putted and missed and then immediately claimed a mulligan due to a playing partner's lack of knowledge of proper golf etiquette. The gentleman became irate and the two started to have a shouting match. Stewie lost that mulligan appeal, but he was not done yet.

On the next hole the gentleman had an unfortunate accident and emitted a loud belch during Stewie's swing. Stewie sliced his drive badly and ran to his bag and pulled out the *Rules of Golf* from his notebook. Yes, Stewie actually referred to an official source on occasion. He found the section concerning distractions and said that noises were a distraction that violated etiquette rules. Just as he finished this point, two attractive women joined the portly man to walk with him on the remaining holes. In order to avoid embarrassment, the gentleman conceded the mulligan.

By the end of this fateful round, Stewie was claiming a rules violation every time the gentleman made the slightest noise whether it was a couch, sneeze, belch, hiccup, or other unnamed sound. Stewie pressed this issue and, probably to avoid the embarrassment of the situation, he was conceded several shots.

It is not known, and Stewie does not say in the notebook, if he won that round. However, the precedent was set for rules involving Stewie-defined etiquette during a round of golf. Stewie liked this one since he knew embarrassment, or the avoidance of embarrassment, could be powerful especially in mixed company and, given his communication skills, he knew he could change the definition of etiquette to fit any situation.

Over the years, true to Stewie's form, he extended this rule to include many more etiquette violations including blinking and breathing. Sadly, the notebook does not contain a story about blinking, so we are on our own to determine its origin.

The Etiquette Mulligan

Etiquette is generally defined as "rules that govern or define socially acceptable behavior." As you must know by now, you need to do these rule definitions. It is your duty to ensure poor behavior by your playing partners does not affect your play on the golf course. Out of all of Stewie's advice, this is probably the one tip you can emulate even in today's modern world of cultural refinement.

Like Stewie, start by pointing out golf etiquette violations to your playing partners. For example, if your worthy competitors walk anywhere on the green, they must have walked across your line. How do they know where you are going to putt? In addition to the obvious golf issues, you can start the round by discussing your concern for the general lack of etiquette in society today. If your playing partners agree with you, or even hint they might sort of agree with you, you should be able to exploit this weakness later.

It is also interesting to note that there is etiquette for virtually every social activity. Etiquette exists for dating, business, wedding planning, dining, and even for writing emails. There is just too much to know for any one person. So assuming you are not playing with an Emily Post junkie, you should be able to speak to this subject more than your playing partners. Look, etiquette is really just good manners. And you are certainly a good judge of manners on the golf course. Right?

Even though the whole etiquette issue is wide open and fertile for your use, we are here to help with a few tips on how to instruct your playing partners on the subtle details concerning proper etiquette. We know you are no Stewie, but give these a try:

- Noise: Literally any noise emitted by someone while you are hitting, putting, lining up your putt, thinking about your next shot, or writing down your birdie for the last hole is a blatant violation of etiquette. Some examples of noise include yelling, talking, whistling, hitting a golf ball with a club, walking, and breathing.

- Blinking: This is mentioned directly in the original lost rule. Although Stewie did not share any stories with us, we know from modern chaos theory that events like a butterfly flapping its wings in the Amazon cause it to rain in Boston. So, obviously, a blinking playing partner can affect the flight of your ball.

- Criticism: If your partners make comments that do not encourage you, you should point out that their insensitivity is poor etiquette. It can cause a break in your normally unbreakable concentration as a result of your lowered self-esteem from that criticism.

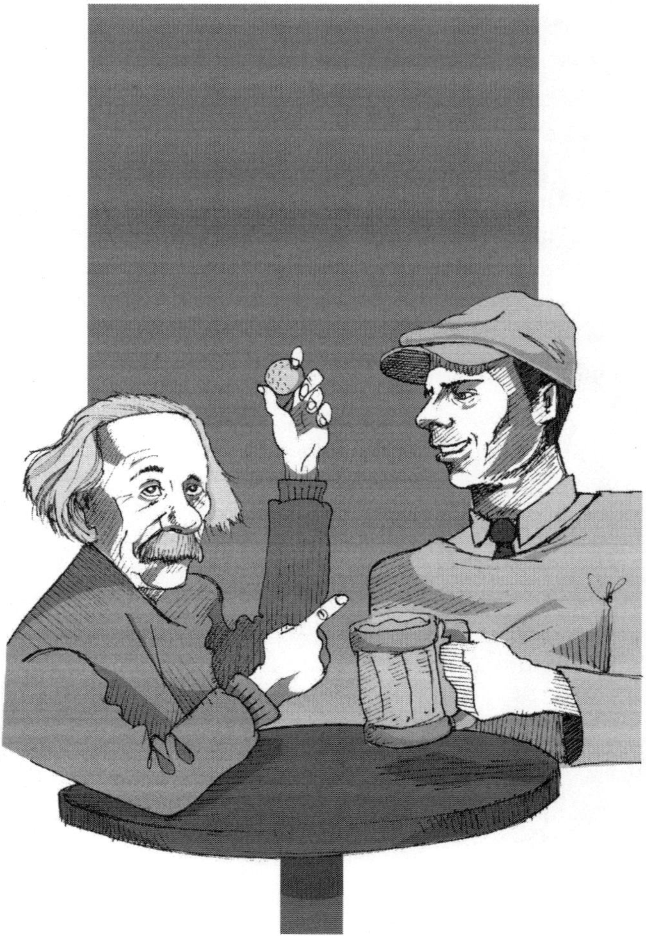

14

Physics of the Golf Ball

Rule 13b.14 *Upon observing a ball that travels in a direction other than desired, the player may inspect the ball to determine if the ball has the correct number of dimples; after determining it does not, which clearly affected the flight of the ball, the player may drop another ball and hit again without penalty.*

One remarkable event that happened in the summer of 1905 adds to the mysterious life of Stewie Mulligan off the golf course. Early one September day, he managed to play a special match. As remarkable as the match was, and the impact it would have on the world, it was curious to see he only made a slight notation in his notebook. "Played with Bill and Al, had interesting discussion at pub with Al on an idea of his."

The match was one that Stewie invited himself to when he heard that a famous inventor named Bill had come to Franklin Park from Ohio. When it was determined that Bill was meeting a man from Switzerland's patent office, Stewie's curiosity peeked and he managed to talk himself into the round with the Franklin Park club pro filling out the foursome.

It turned out that Bill was none other than William Taylor who had just patented the idea of dimples on a golf ball. The man from the patent office in Switzerland was actually a German who knew a little about physics and wanted to talk to Mr. Taylor.

While this may be interesting, it is what happened after the round that added to Stewie's reputation for a keen mind. It seems that Bill had to catch a train early in the evening and the club pro had a dinner date. So Al and Stewie went off to dinner at a pub to celebrate Stewie's victory—you must have known by now that Stewie would have won the match. As was recorded by an eavesdropping local reporter in a blurb in the Dorchester News the next day, Al and Stewie spent the night arguing Albert's idea for a new theory in physics—not that it is relative to golf.

The Dimple Mulligan

While it is likely that the closest to anything Einstein you will get is seeing a book about him in the bookstore on your way to read *Golf Digest*, imagine the impact you could have on your score if your playing partners think you are some sort of genius like Albert.

Now you need to focus on this next section as it can be mentally challenging. Stewie has these notations in an appendix to his notebook. We have added several modern references and updated some of the golfing facts to current rules. Use this information when appropriate to impress your competitors and raise their GA.

Golf Ball Facts

Although we say in Chapter 6 that you should not use the golf ball for an equipment issue, perhaps we were wrong—we know you are shocked at that possibility. However, if you are able to establish your expertise beyond any doubt with your opponents, or they are dumber than sliced bread—oops, sorry to use the "s" word—then you may have a chance to blame the ball after all.

You should establish your superior knowledge by preparing the foursome early by peppering the conversation with facts on the golf ball. Then, when you really need to explain how your ball drifted into the woods, you can point to an imperfection of the ball. Perhaps it violates rules governing golf ball construction. Just the fact that you know these details will probably amaze your foursome. They are as follows:

- Weight of golf ball is 1.620 oz or 45.93 gm

- Diameter of golf ball is 1.68 in or 42.67 mm
- There are 330-500 dimples

Use the metric system when playing with Canadians, Asians, Australians, Europeans, or Antarcticans (basically anyone but Americans) to impress them that you are international in your education and knowledge.

While the weight and size are good choices in most cases, the number of dimples is sure to succeed. You can claim the ball is defective and the number of dimples is an odd number (virtually all balls have an even number of dimples). Begin by slowly (we mean very slowly) counting the dimples and, especially if it is late in the day, near lunch time, or near happy hour, your partners are likely to give up and concede the mulligan.

Magnus Force

We would explain this rule of physics here but would you really understand it? Just accept that the Magnus Force rule means the speed of a spinning golf ball is different on each side of the ball as it flies through the air. Thus, any imperfection in your ball may affect the travel of the ball.

Use the rule if your playing partner says, "Didn't Clint Eastwood star in that movie?"

Skip it if your partner says "I think lift and drag are more important than the leading air pressure on the opposite side of the spinning ball" or anything that sounds like that.

If you do not have a sharp mind, you can assist your memory by writing these facts on a note card that you carry in your wallet. If your eyesight is still good, you might try writing the facts on a golf tee. That way, you can start each hole by discussing a golf fact, thus enhancing your chances of using a Stewie rule on that hole. Remember, it is about sincerity and credibility. By the way, if you don't have a sharp mind and decent eyesight, what are you doing on the golf course anyway?

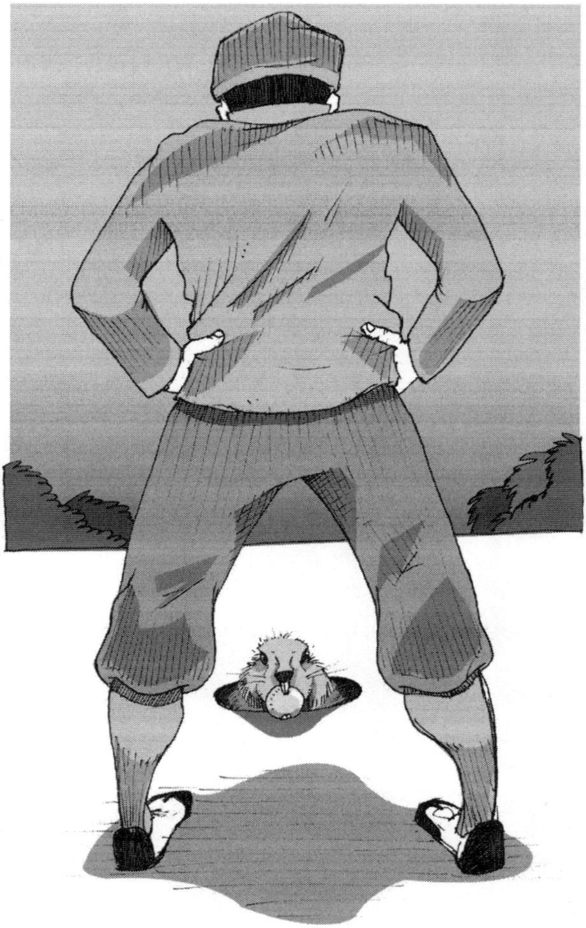

15

Animal Kingdom

Rule 13b.15 Upon arriving at a hidden green and not being able to locate the ball, and upon asserting that the ball was removed by a gopher as there is no other explanation for the ball not lying adjacent to the hole, the player may drop a ball within a club length of the hole and hit again without penalty.

Perhaps the most interesting story about Stewie in his later years involves his supposed use of a gopher to help him with his rules interpretations. The notebook only has one reference to an animal and it is only found in the rule shown above. It appears that as Stewie grew older and his golfing skills diminished, his rules creativity flourished.

While no official evidence exists, Lewie J. conducted extensive research via interviews with descendants of Franklin Park members to learn as much as possible about these rumors. In fact, it appears that no one agrees on a single story regarding use of the "gopher exception," but they all agree that Stewie used it often—particularly when he was losing.

The basic story lines all point to times when Stewie was losing late in the round. He would hit a shot to a green that could not be seen until the golfers arrive at it. When they do, Stewie's ball cannot be seen, but a gopher is sitting next to the green. Stewie claims the gopher ate his ball and he is entitled to a drop where the ball should have been. Stewie walks close to the hole and finds what he calls a ball mark. He then drops a ball within a club length of the "mark."

Although many stories claim Stewie had trained the gopher to take his ball and hide it and mark the green, this cannot be proven. One old friend of Stewie's claimed the gopher was artificial and Stewie told his partners the gopher had rabies to keep them away. Whatever the truth, it is one of the many folklore stories about our friendly Irish golfer.

The Gopher Mulligan

We will assume here you are no Dr. Doolittle and cannot have a gopher at the ready. We also will assume you do not really care much about gopher eating habits, behavior patterns, etc. Therefore, we need to provide you with just enough knowledge and a few tips to help you in this situation. By the way, if you really do care that much about gophers, we don't want to know!

By now, you should know something about your playing partners. If they are avid environmentalists or conservationists, you might try distracting them early as a set up for the Gopher Mulligan. You can try, for example, to note how awful it was for the gopher in *Caddyshack* to have been mistreated. If, amazingly, you sense an opportunity here, you need to be ready when you reach the green and cannot find your ball.

The key is to change the discussion of how you cannot find your ball to how sad it is that the golf course has infringed on the habitat of the local gopher community. Talk fast and low and show as much emotion as you can (if you are not a gopher lover, try picturing yourself buying the drinks after you lose this round).

If you are playing with a somewhat intelligent person, it might make sense to ensure there are actually gophers in the area. If you are not sure, a quick check with the greens keeping staff can help you especially if you need to identify an animal to substitute. Be smart about this however, as you don't want to say something like "I am sympathetic to infringing on termite habitat since they are so cute and furry."

If your partners are the other extreme, and say, they spent the first three holes discussing how to kill all the wildlife they have seen, then you need to take a radically different approach. Start with statements such as "I hate those gophers that ruin this beautiful golf course" and "The only good gopher is a dead gopher." The latter statement will come in handy when you feign outrage that the gopher you saw run away with your golf ball cannot be shot on the spot. You will know you have pulled it off when your playing partners offer sympathy (or a gun) and tell you to drop another ball with no penalty.

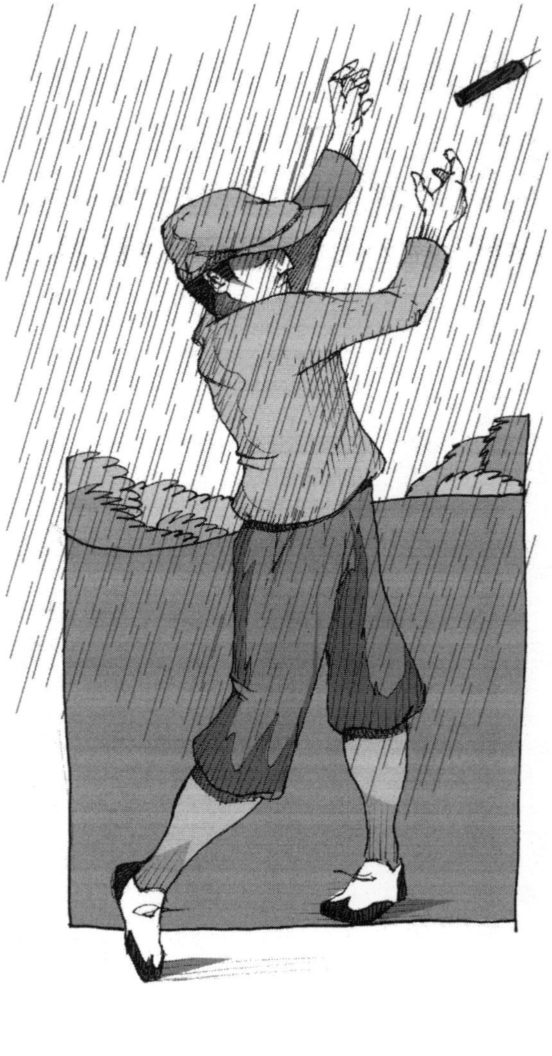

16

Mother Nature

> Rule 13b.16 *Upon striking the ball and the player making a determination that the shot was mis-hit by such player due to a specifically identifiable weather disturbance, the player may drop a ball no closer to the hole, and hit again without penalty.*

As we know, Stewie was no stranger to the challenges of Mother Nature. From his homeland in Ireland to the blast furnace summers of Africa to the oppressive humidity in the South American rain forests to the bitter New England winters, Stewie had seen it all and in most cases played in it as well.

When Stewie first played at Franklin Park, it was a beautiful spring day. He could not believe his good fortune as he recalled the squalls he had seen in his home country. He played well that day and was immediately looking forward to his next round. Apparently he kept going on and on about how beautiful the weather was to the point that his playing partners finally told him something to the effect that "You ain't seen nothing yet!" Stewie had no idea what they meant that day.

Stewie had been traveling around New England doing some odd jobs during that first summer in Boston, and so he was not able to return to Franklin Park until early autumn. He rode to the course with great expectation despite the graying, dark skies and the rising winds. When he arrived at the course, the wind cut right through him and the first spittle of rain hit his brow. It was not to be the last.

Stewie teed off with his group in the biting wind and the ever increasing rain. By the third hole, there was no blue left in the sky, the wind was approaching epic proportions, and the rain was now coming down in sheets. Golf umbrellas were pointless as the winds whipped the rain around so it was now coming almost straight at the golfers. Needless to say (but if we didn't say it there would be no book) the playing conditions were miserable. It was nearly impossible to hold a club much less hit a good shot.

Inspiration struck Stewie just as he tried to hit a five iron into a small green. Given the slipperiness of his grip due to the weather, the club flew out of his hands. It went straight towards one of his playing partners, just missing him. The man at first was sure that Stewie was aiming at him since he had won the prior hole, but soon realized it was an honest mistake.

While Stewie's Flying Five Iron was the initial inspiration for him to create what today we know as the Weather Mulligan, over the years he broadened the scope of the rule to include a variety of weather-inspired events. Fortunately, the Boston weather provided great fodder for Stewie to do this.

The Weather Mulligan

Today, golfers all over the world have been given a tremendous opportunity to invoke the Weather Mulligan on a heretofore unprecedented level. This opportunity can be summed up in two words: Global Warming.

Some say it is the only identifiable benefit of it. Even those golfers who do not believe there is any such thing have been known to invoke the Weather Mulligan citing it as the basis for using it. Don't worry about the scientific basis for it, just trust us.

Today, together with the power of instant information, golfers all over the World can invoke the Weather Mulligan for such things as massive hurricanes, El Nino, La Nina, the Gulf Stream (not to be confused with Gulfstream private jets for rich golfers), and mudslides. However, the granddaddy of all Weather Mulligans is Global Warming.

If your ball lands in the first several inches of rough off the fairway, you may invoke the Weather Mulligan by declaring that, due to Global Warming, the levels of the world's oceans are increasing thereby stimulating the growth of natural grasses as found on golf courses around the world thus resulting in rough being where fairways used to be. Therefore, your ball would have been in the fairway as you had planned had it not been for increased growth of grass due to Global Warming. Consequently, you may drop another ball in the fairway and hit again without penalty. For additional applications of specific weather-related mulligans, please refer to the Emergency Mulligan List.

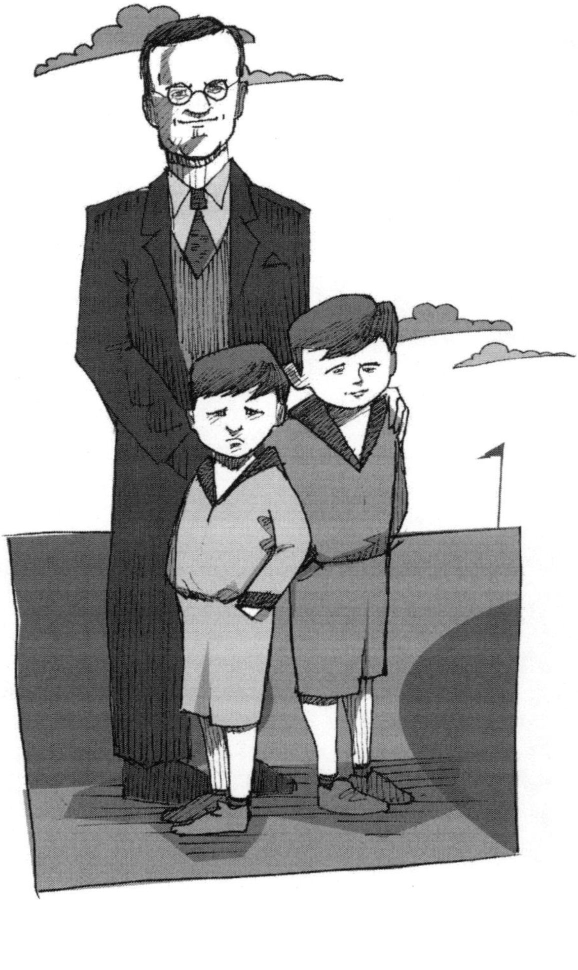

17

Those Who Master Words

> Rule 13b.17 *Upon striking the ball, the player makes a determination that such shot did not land in the middle of the fairway or in the middle of the green, the player may drop a ball no closer to the hole and hit again without penalty.*

Not much is known about Stewie's personal life after he married. We do know that he had several children and word was that he really liked teaching kids to play golf. Rumor also had it that he would even take children out on the course on the odd occasion they arrived at Franklin Park.

One afternoon Stewie went to the course and was looking for a group to join. He was only able to find one man looking for a partner for only nine holes. It was getting late in the day, so Stewie reluctantly agreed to play for nine. Just then, two small children came running out of the clubhouse to join their father.

After a few holes, Stewie and the father decided to let the children try to play. There was no one behind them and a slow foursome in front of them. The father then spent most of his time teaching the older of the sons. This left Stewie time to teach little Jack.

It was an interesting few hours in that the father kept up a running dialog with his sons telling them story after story about people in both Boston and national politics. Each successive story seemed more amazing than the one before it. He kept using analogies of "finding middle ground to get things done." Fortunately for Stewie, the father could not find any middle ground in a fairway, so he easily won the small wager with Mr. Kennedy.

This story would not be that interesting except for one small event. Stewie walked up to one of the last holes and hit his drive just as the sun began to set with a full moon beginning to rise. This turned out to be one of his longer drives of the round. The young boy yelled enthusiastically, "Mr. Mulligan, you hit that ball all the way to the moon! Let's go get it."

For the last few holes, the boy talked about nothing else but going to the moon. He was fascinated with the idea and asked Stewie if they could go when he grew up.

Stewie smiled and told him, "It would take an act of a President of the United States to start a program to send a man to the moon." Stewie noted in his journal that the boy was serious and contemplative the rest of the round.

The Political Mulligan

Some say that politics in the United States in the early 21st century has become extremely divisive. The folks who say that clearly have not studied the history of American politics. For example, one of the closest races in American presidential elections occurred in the year '00 when the Vice President and supporter of a Governor Clinton lost a close and contested election. No, not that election. This one was in 1800 between Aaron Burr and Thomas Jefferson.

Tom's friend Alexander had, shall we say, an adversarial relationship with the new Vice President (in those days the loser in the election became the Vice President—imagine that today!) Their disagreement deteriorated to a duel, in which Burr shot and killed Hamilton. After the duel, Burr ran off to form his own country and Alex ended up on our $10 bill—which reminds us, we need to get back to mulligans so you can keep those Hamiltons in your wallet.

Today, much like the early 1800s, politics raise emotions in almost everyone. Since dueling between political foes is no longer legal (a sad day for American politics), we are reduced to yelling, pointing fingers, and complaining. Um, sounds like your golf game, right?

So, how do you take this rich history and make it help your golf score—you thought we'd never get there, we know. Remember that Rule 13b.17 speaks to the "middle of" the fairway and green. Unfortunately, it seems these days that no one is in the middle of the road. The good news is politics and golf have much in common. Let's look to the political world for some lessons to use in our golf game:

Adaptability

It is important to know which way the wind is blowing to know how far right or how far left to go.

Trusted Advisors

Politicians have a media advisors, policy advisors, and legal advisors. Their collective job is to create a good image, advise on actions to take, ensure their boss always wins, and keep their boss out of jail. Basically, it's the same job as your caddie.

Gullibility Assessment

Perhaps no one depends more than Stewie on a gullible audience than do politicians.

Mulligans

You know these are the key to your success. Politicians also have a mulligan if they lose an election. They can run again. And again. And again.

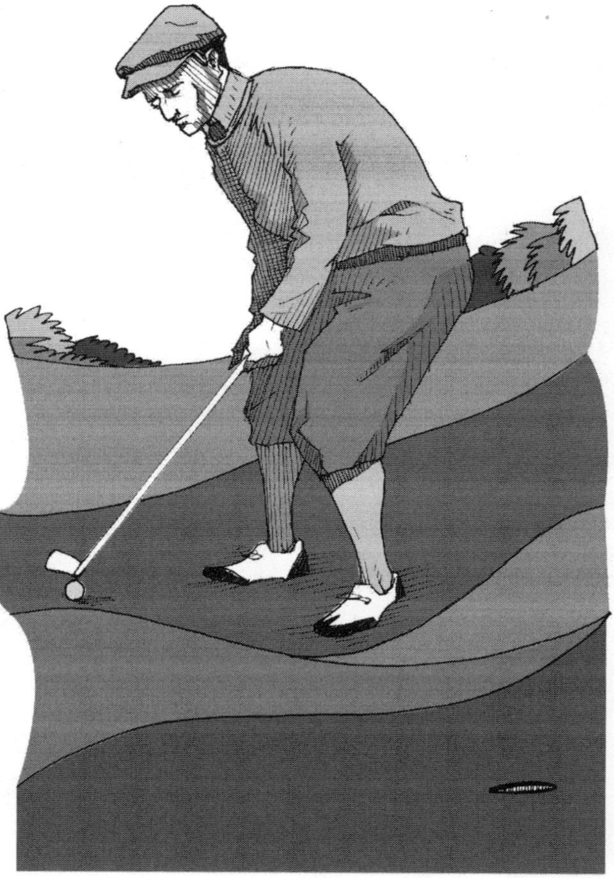

18

Last Resort

Rule 13b.18 *Upon determining that a player is in danger of losing the round when starting the final hole and that player is clearly superior in all facets of the game and a less than optimal shot is struck, the player may drop another ball and hit again until the shot is as desired, without penalty.*

It was rare that Stewie approached the 18th hole with the match not already conceded by his playing partners. Either he had beaten the opponents outright—something that actually happened fairly often—or he had skillfully used his rules to ensure victory. In some cases the opponents had conceded because they either had enough of the rules interpretations or they decided the pure entertainment value of Stewie's rule interpretations was enough to buy him a drink or two.

There were those rare cases, however, where Stewie was standing over the 18th tee with the match seemingly lost or at least gravely in doubt. Yet, his journal only mentions seventeen losses over his career. This is a remarkable feat, if true, given he played virtually every day for over twenty years.

We know the 18th hole at Franklin Park was well suited for Stewie's game. It is rumored that he made subtle changes in the slope of the green around the hole locations that only he knew about. Since he maintained a relationship with the grounds keeping staff after he retired from the job, it is possible these course modifications were continued.

In any event, Stewie was able to use the old double-or-nothing trick most times given his confidence in winning the 18th hole. If partners would not give him this opportunity, he stated several times in his notebook, he felt obliged to use any rule interpretation at his disposal to combat their lack of sportsmanship.

The Desperation Mulligan

If you have correctly used the previous seventeen rules, it is unlikely you will find yourself in need of a Desperation Mulligan. But let's assume your playing partner's GA was a little lower than you would have liked, and you were unable to use Stewie's rules to your advantage. Maybe your partners were skilled competitors who have honed their game over many hours of toil and sweat on the practice range. Or perhaps, you really are that bad!

One of the keys to this rule is to ensure you have worn down your opponents over the course of the round. They need to be pretty dull at this point or ready to do anything to make you quit pleading your case and your rule interpretations.

The list below summarizes the many final hole rule enhancements directly from Stewie's notebook. Note: Use these carefully as your partners might believe that you are pushing your luck.

Combinations and Omissions

The obvious place to start is to use any rule from the *Book of Mulligan* which you have not already used. If you are so bad that you have used all of them by now, then you might try combining some of the rules. Some potential combinations are as follows:

> Water-Sand Mulligan: Both water and sand are under the grass on the tee box, under the grass in the fairway, and under the green. Go ahead and give it a try.

Clothing-Equipment Mulligan: Since you are now on the 18th hole, you must have some mud, dirt, lint, something on your clothing or clubs. This should be reason enough for this mulligan.

Political-Weather Mulligan: Weatherman and politicians, need we say more?

Gopher-Dimple Mulligan: Use the fact that gophers have dimples to claim a two shot mulligan—okay this is really a stretch.

Injury

If all else fails and you have absolutely no chance of winning, then you can exaggerate an injury you have, had once, or might get one day. This will allow you to withdraw from the match and invalidate the results. It is also helpful to gain you sympathy in the clubhouse once you manage to limp back. Several example injuries that cannot be seen but will definitely cause your play to degrade include the pulled left toe, strained ear lobe, blurred vision (obviously the reason you missed the last five putts), and the post hair partum syndrome.

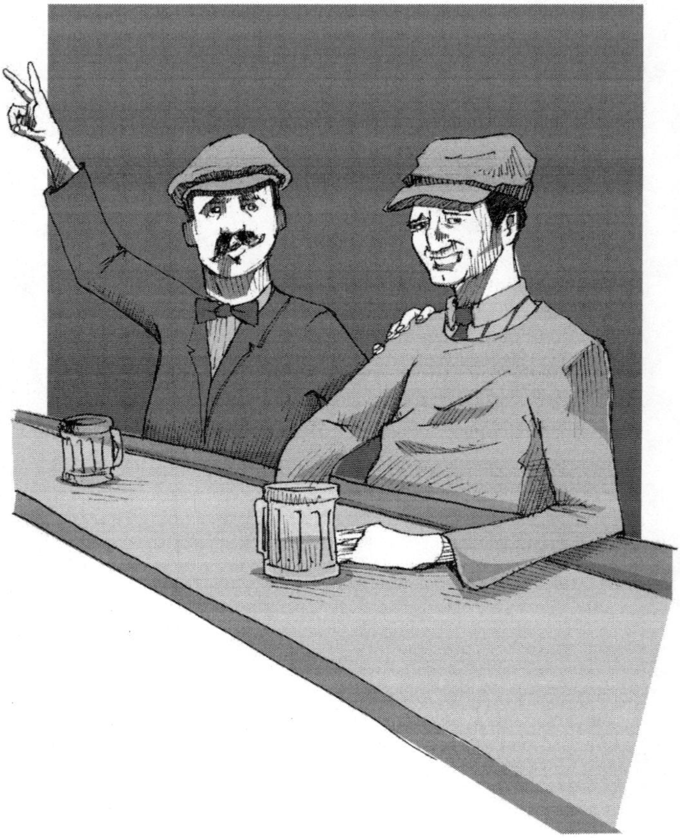

19

All Good Things …

> Rule 13b.19 *Upon completion of the round, the player with the highest number of recorded strokes will purchase the liquid refreshments for their foursome at the clubhouse.*

The 19th Hole is traditionally a place to meet and reflect on the exciting round just completed. If, as in the case with Stewie, wagers were made, it is the time to settle up. As we have said, Stewie rarely, if ever, had to pay. While it is not known what wagers Stewie placed, it is known that most players did not seem angry or hesitant to settle. You see, Stewie really was a nice guy.

As you know by now, Stewie was an accomplished golfer in his own right. He likely won most matches without the use of Rule 13b. When he did require just that little assistance, he was evidently able to do it in a way that most people found acceptable if not amusing.

So it was a rare occasion indeed when Stewie had to resort to the super secret, highly classified Lost Rule 13b-123. It appears from stories we found in researching this book, that if Stewie was not able to use enough mulligans to win the round, he had one last trick—and you thought the Desperation Mulligan was his last chance!

Unfortunately, this option was so secret that Stewie destroyed it late in his life. Sorry, but we can't solve all your problems!

Know Your Priorities

One of the problems with today's society is that we are always in a hurry. Rush to a meeting. Grab the cell phone. And, unbelievably, use the Blackberry to read email while on the golf course or in the clubhouse.

Listen folks, the golf course is a sacred place. It is not to be corrupted with mobile phones, Blackberrys or anything of such capability. While it is permissible to conduct business on the course, this must be done in a strange and unfamiliar way: talking face-to-face!

Once the round is over, take time to further bond with your foursome. Patch up any differences or disagreements. This is especially true if you used Stewie's rules and are enjoying free lunch and a beer. Go ahead and make that friendly gesture toward the now humbled losers in your group. Offer to play them again.

If by some miracle you lost (obviously you need to study this book more), be humble and compliment your opponent's game. Remember that good sportsmanship is important. You also want to begin immediately to rebuild their belief that you are sincere. (See Chapter 1—Get Off to a Good Start).

Of course, that is not enough, so we have even more advice if you lost. And this is free just for buying this book! The lesson for you is to set your priorities. While it may be important to win, it is more important to win the drinks at the 19th hole. For example, a master plan would be to creatively arrange to lose to your boss but win the drinks from the other players.

The key to this success is in the planning stage. While on the practice range and putting green, you must craft a set of bets that ultimately are so confusing only you can decipher who won what at the end of the round. Since you will have successfully used Stewie's notebook to lower your boss's score so that he or she is happy, it is unlikely the boss will realize or even care how your bet interpretations caused someone else in the group to pay.

No matter how your round turned out, playing golf is better than just about anything else you do. Okay, maybe not everything else you do! But, whether you win or lose, you must have fun on the golf course. We hope you enjoyed the advice from our old Irish friend. So as you lift your glass, always give a silent "cheers" to Stewart J. Mulligan and thank him for his wisdom!

Emergency Mulligan List

Although one would think that eighteen mulligans would be enough to guarantee your lower score, if you play like us, we know you need more!

These Emergency Mulligans may also come in handy if you play with the same partners more than once.

Or, for the more ambitious of players, you can reference this list to try to use more than one mulligan on a single hole. Accomplish this and you become a Mulligan Grandmaster. That is the standard that would make Stewie proud.

Weather Mulligans

Unpredictable Weather Mulligan

If the weather forecaster, or meteorologist, makes an incorrect weather prediction, you are entitled to three mulligans since you were unprepared for the change. Unless you live in Los Angeles where it is 72 degrees everyday, you can use this pretty much anywhere and any day. If you don't like three mulligans, be unpredictable yourself and chose another number.

Hurricane Mulligan

You can take one or more mulligans per round depending upon the category of the hurricane. One mulligan per category. For example, a category five hurricane will result in five mulligans for that round. You may want to consider not playing during a hurricane.

Tornado Mulligan

Similarly, the player may qualify for one or more mulligans depending upon the strength of the tornado on the Fujita scale (F0-F5). Also, if you can prove it to your playing partners, a nearby "Wizard of Oz" tornado (F6) enables you to claim six mulligans for any one round. You may want to consider taking shelter if you see a tornado.

Lightning Mulligan

You can take as many mulligans per round as you see lightning strikes. No one is going to argue with you if you invoke a Lightning Mulligan as most normal, intelligent people will be nowhere near the golf course at this point. You should definitely head to a shelter if you see lightning. You don't always get a mulligan if you are hit by lightning.

Thunder Mulligan

Only one mulligan per round as once you hear this you should be getting your backside off the course as soon as possible. See Lightning Mulligan above for additional information.

Snow Mulligan

If you play golf in the snow, you don't deserve a mulligan.

Personality Mulligans

Type A Personality Mulligan

Take as many Mulligans as you want as you are probably a jerk and most people who play with you don't really enjoy it. Note: they may be trying to get the round over as quickly as possible, so no one really wants to argue about your true score.

Senior Moment Mulligan

One Mulligan per round. If you forget, just take another one. Particularly effective for golfers over 70 years old. Who's going to argue? Just don't try this when it comes time to paying off your golf bets.

Seasonal Mulligans

Spring Mulligan

One mulligan per round during this season until you have played enough practice rounds to restore your form—whatever that is. But then again, you never really get enough practice so use it all season.

Summer Mulligan

Two mulligans per round as it is hotter now and the heat drains you.

Fall Mulligan

Three Mulligans per round as you are probably losing balls under leaves that have fallen from the trees into the middle of the fairway—or close to the fairway where you always hit your ball.

Winter Mulligan

If it is warm in the winter where you play, good for you. Try using cold excuses such as my finely tuned muscles don't work as well in the cold. If you live in a truly cold climate, try taking up watching reruns on the Golf Channel. Or maybe watch that video of golf lessons you bought yourself years ago. If it is snowing, see Snow Mulligan.

Celebrity Mulligans

Oprah Mulligan

Let's all sit around the green and have a deep emotional discussion about the stress of not getting your mulligan. Then we can all cry, laugh, and cheer or jump up and down on the nearest couch. Sometimes someone gives out expensive gifts so we will want to do it again, and we forget about the mulligan.

Jerry Springer Mulligan

If you don't get a mulligan you want by telling a story no one believes, three very large guys will beat you up and hit you with a chair. Oops, that is the Geraldo Mulligan.

Stephen King Mulligan

You get this mulligan if you can tell a scary story about what happened to the golfers who did not give someone a well-deserved mulligan.

William Shakespeare Mulligan

To take a mulligan or not take a mulligan, that is the question. Actually, there is no question. Take the mulligan.

Franklin Roosevelt Mulligan

The only thing we have to fear is fear of not getting our mulligan.

John F. Kennedy Mulligan

Ask not what you can do for your mulligan; ask what your mulligan can do for you.

Benjamin Franklin Mulligan

A mulligan saved is a mulligan earned.

Charles Dickens Mulligan

It was the best of times; it was the worst of times. It was time to take a mulligan.

Geography Mulligans

Hemisphere Mulligan

You may have heard that the water in a toilet spins opposite ways in the northern and southern hemispheres. Since you have this knowledge, there are at least two ways you can use this mulligan. First, and perhaps most believable, all golf balls spin. If your ball is consistently going the wrong way, you should claim this mulligan for the first few holes until you learn which way the spin works in the hemisphere you are playing in. Second, for putts, if you keep pulling (we mean just barely missing) a putt, you can claim a mulligan until you learn how the spinning ball off your putter reacts in this hemisphere. Note that this mulligan is easier to claim if you actually have changed hemispheres from where you usually play.

High Altitude Mulligan

In the thin air of the mountains, like Denver, Colorado, or any location not adjacent to the ocean, the spin you normally put on your ball might not work as you have intended. Therefore, if your ball takes flight off the fairway, it must be due to thin air. If you live in Denver and play somewhere else, then claim the opposite: the air thickness made your perfectly applied spin move the ball more than normal.

European Union Mulligan

First get ten foursomes that have nothing in common. Then convince them they should all play by the same rules, for the same bets, and that the other foursomes get to determine these. Then wait five years before you actually take the mulligan.

Canadian Mulligan

You should be able to get several mulligans from a nice Canadian, eh? Just make sure he is not a hockey player when you ask.

Scottish Mulligan

If you have ever played golf in Scotland, you cannot take a mulligan. Ever. For tradition's sake.

Tokyo Mulligan

It is so expensive to play golf in Tokyo, that if you can afford to play golf there, you can definitely afford to take a mulligan.

Musical Mulligans

Beetles Mulligan

The musical world's most famous foursome. You get a mulligan if your name is John, Paul, George, or Ringo. Or if you know someone named Ringo.

Country Music Mulligan

You crashed your pickup, lost your woman, and your dog ran away. You deserve a mulligan.

Country Music Mulligan #2

Your Cheatin' Partners need to give you a break or you will leave them. However, depending on how much you have pushed Rule 13b, be careful before you try to use this one.

Johnny Cash Mulligan

You get a mulligan if you have been in Folsom Prison. If you play it right, you should get as many mulligans as prisons you have been in.

Reggae Mulligan

Ya mon. Ya need a mulligon.

More Political Mulligans

Vice Presidential Mulligan

Actually there is no Vice Presidential Mulligan, since no one pays any attention to what a Vice President does anyway.

Republican Mulligan

This is for times you hit the ball too far to the right.

Democratic Mulligan

This is for times you hit the ball too far to the left.

Libertarian Mulligan

Since the Libertarian Party believes in minimal regulation, there really are no rules for invoking this mulligan. You have free will, generally unfettered by regulation. Exercise it.

The Green Party Mulligan

Since the Green Party is socially and environmentally conscious, your use of this mulligan also must be thoughtful and equally conscious. If this is too much trouble, which it is for most golfers, just pick one of the other mulligans and have a party on the green.

Govenator Mulligan

If you happen to be lucky enough to live in a state where the governor has a cool nickname (note that prison numbers don't count as nicknames), then you can try to get your foursome laughing at your bad jokes such as "that ball went in the hole like Jesse the Body Ventura slammed it in" or "As for my bad shots, I will terminate them." We don't know how you get a mulligan directly from all of this, but bad humor might help you when you later talk seriously about the *Book of Mulligan* rules.

Dictator Mulligan

This is the most powerful mulligan. A dictator may, as the title implies, dictate his or her score at any point before, during or after the match. Usually requires military support.

Presidential Mulligan

Taken throughout the years by the Presidents of the United States, this is one mulligan no one argues with and may be taken as many times as the President so chooses.

The Socialist Party Mulligan

Since the Socialist Party believes we are all in this together, you can only use this mulligan if you also let every one of your playing partners use the mulligan at the same time. What fun is that?

The Communist Party Mulligan

Since the Communist Party believes from each according to their ability, to each according to their needs, you now know why there are no great Communist golfers and, as a result, no Communist Party Mulligan. What's the point?

Corporate Mulligans

Enron Mulligan

Numbers can always be "adjusted" to show you in the best light. Use this any way you wish but remember not to send any emails about it.

CEO Mulligan

This has been taken for years by many CEOs in companies worldwide; remember golf is truly a global game. More recently, if the CEO has had their company restate its financials more than once in the prior twelve months, then the CEO may take the same number of mulligans per round as the number of financial restatements. After all, how could anyone expect them to keep their golf score any more accurately than their company's financials?

Founder Mulligan

People who start companies are a different breed. They rarely believe anyone else really has a clue about the business they have started. They always think they know best. On the golf course, a Founder Mulligan can only be invoked by such a person. Since they always believe they know best, they can use this mulligan at any point during the round and for any reason, since, as we said, they always know what is best.

Big Company Mulligan

In contrast to the Founder Mulligan, the Big Company Mulligan can only be used by a person who works at a Fortune Global 1000 Company. If you don't know what that is, then you aren't a Big Company person and may not invoke this mulligan. Of course, in Big Companies there are rules and procedures that any employee must follow before anything can get done. Moreover, since using a mulligan is a deviation from the standard process, it requires an exception. Exception processing takes longer and costs more so it should be used only in very serious circumstances. Due to this result, Six Sigma was actually invented to identify root causes, test corrections, implement them, and test again. They say all of this results in a faster process. We have no idea, but playing with a Big Company Person who tries to invoke the Big Company Mulligan can be a long and trying process. We suggest you avoid these players if at all possible.

Notice this is the longest, most confusing explanation of any mulligan.

Chapter 11 Mulligan

Any company that employs lessons learned from this book should not have to file Chapter 11. However, be careful when you use other methods of bookkeeping. See Enron Mulligan.

Wal-Mart Mulligan

To guarantee the lowest score possible, offshore your game to China. Tip your caddie almost nothing.

Neiman Marcus Mulligan

When you have the highest score in your foursome, it is time to take this mulligan. Simply choose a number of mulligans that is not believable, just like the price of the blue jeans your spouse just bought at Neiman Marcus.

The Final Word

Tiger Woods Mulligan

You're kidding, right?

The Lost Rule 13b

Rule 13b *If after due consideration of playing the ball as it lies, and the player determines the lie of the ball is not optimum, or would not be if the ball was found, the player may consider several factors leading to the lie as shown in Rule 13b subsections, thus allowing the player to drop another ball and play without penalty.*

Rule 13b.1 *Upon striking the ball on the 1st tee and determining that the ball has not come to rest in a desirable location, the player may tee up and hit another ball without penalty.*

Rule 13b.2 *Upon arriving at a water hazard and discovering the ball has entered the hazard, and, after declaring to your playing partners a sincere belief that the ball had not entered the hazard, the player may drop another ball and hit again without penalty.*

Rule 13b.3 *Upon observing the flight of the struck ball where it is determined that a player's wallet has affected the player's finely tuned balance, the player may remove the wallet, drop another ball, and hit again without penalty.*

Rule 13b.4 *Upon arriving to find the ball is not located in the center of the fairway, and determining that there is a sprinkler head within fifty yards of the ball, the player may assert that the ball hit the sprinkler head and move the ball into the center of the fairway and hit again without penalty.*

Rule 13b.5 *Upon observing a putted ball that takes an unexplained break, and the player determines that a mild earthquake just occurred, even if not all playing partners felt the earth shaking, or you are within 1000 miles of California, the player may putt again without penalty.*

Rule 13b.6 *Upon observing the flight of a well struck ball which goes astray, resembling a hook or a slice, when it is determined that the player rarely, if ever, hits a hook or a slice, the player may inspect his club to determine if it has a defect, and, finding a defect, may drop a ball, choose another club, and hit again without penalty.*

Rule 13b.7 *Upon striking a shot that does not travel in the intended direction and upon a determination by the player that an article of clothing interfered with the player's natural swing motion, the player may drop a ball and hit again without penalty.*

Rule 13b.8 *Upon striking a ball in a sand trap and the ball lands either in the same sand trap, a different sand trap, or in any location other than on the intended green, the player may elect to drop a ball no closer to the hole and hit again without penalty.*

Rule 13b.9 *Upon striking a shot that does not travel the intended distance, and upon a determination by the player that said player is hungry or thirsty thus exhibiting signs of dangerously low blood sugar that clearly impairs said player's physical capability, the player may elect to drop a ball no closer to the hole, consume some combination of food and liquids, and hit again without penalty.*

Rule 13b.10 *Upon completion of the first nine holes of an eighteen hole round, when the player determines that their cumulative score for said nine holes exceeds the score intended by said player, the player may, at their sole discretion, adjust said Front 9 score by one or more strokes in order to better align said player's actual score with their intended score without penalty.*

Rule 13b.11 *Upon striking the ball in less than an optimal manner, and upon a determination by the player that such sub-optimal striking of the ball resulted from a distraction caused by an insect, such as a killer bee, the player may, at their sole discretion, drop a ball and hit again without penalty.*

Rule 13b.12 *Upon striking a ball and, upon a determination by the player that such shot did not travel in its intended normal, straight and long trajectory, and upon further determination that the cause of such misdirection was tears that filled the player's eyes from missing a six-inch putt on the prior green, or other equal tragedy, the player may wipe their eyes, drop another ball, and hit again without penalty.*

Rule 13b.13 *Upon striking the ball with less than the desired results, and upon determining that one of your playing partners has violated the rules of golf etiquette during your swing such as coughing, sneezing, blinking, or breathing, the player may drop another ball and hit again without penalty.*

Rule 13b.14 *Upon observing a ball that travels in a direction other than desired, the player may inspect the ball to determine if the ball has the correct number of dimples; after determining it does not, which clearly affected the flight of the ball, the player may drop another ball and hit again without penalty.*

Rule 13b.15 *Upon arriving at a hidden green and not being able to locate the ball, and upon asserting that the ball was removed by a gopher as there is no other explanation for the ball not lying adjacent to the hole, the player may drop a ball within a club length of the hole and hit again without penalty.*

Rule 13b.16 *Upon striking the ball and the player making a determination that the shot was mis-hit by such player due to a specifically identifiable weather disturbance, the player may drop a ball no closer to the hole, and hit again without penalty.*

Rule 13b.17 *Upon striking the ball, the player makes a determination that such shot did not land in the middle of the fairway or in the middle of the green, the player may drop a ball no closer to the hole and hit again without penalty.*

Rule 13b.18 *Upon determining that a player is in danger of losing the round when starting the final hole and that player is clearly superior in all facets of the game and a less than optimal shot is struck, the player may drop another ball and hit again until the shot is as desired, without penalty.*

Rule 13b.19 *Upon completion of the round, the player with the highest number of recorded strokes will purchase the liquid refreshments for their foursome at the clubhouse.*

Submit your favorite mulligan to:

myfavorite@bookofmulligan.com

to Enter Contests and Win Gifts.

Buy merchandise such as hats, shirts, ball markers, and copies of the lost Rule 13b

Visit www.bookofmulligan.com

978-0-595-44427-4
0-595-44427-X

Made in the USA